Walking from
Garstang and Wyresdale

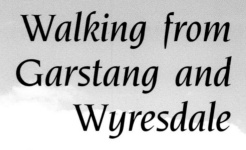

Walking from
Garstang and
Wyresdale

Ian and Krysia Brodie

First published in 1986, fifth edition 2008
by Palatine Books,
Carnegie House,
Chatsworth Road
Lancaster LA1 4SL
www.palatinebooks.com

British Library Cataloguing-in-Publication data
A catalogue record for this book is available from the British Library

ISBN: 978-1-874181-50-7

Designed and typeset by Carnegie Book Production
www.carnegiebookproduction.com

Printed and bound in the UK by Alden Press

Contents

Introduction

Welcome to the fifth edition of *Walking from Garstang*. The first edition appeared in 1986 and partially owed its origins to various editions of *Forty Rambles* by Bruce Clucas, the doyen of Preston walkers from the 1930s to the 1960s, of which Ian was privileged to produce the seventh and final edition. The various editions of that book, which appeared from 1933, helped many Lancashire ramblers' explore their local countryside, not least the area of the River Brock and the River Wyre.

This edition is new in that each of the walks in the previous editions has undergone some modification, new stiles and fences for example, quickly change the information in the book. Please be aware that changes may have occurred between preparing this edition and the time of your walk.

The 66 km (41 mile) Wyre Way footpath, the idea of Wyre Borough Council is covered by the first nine circular walks of the book thus enabling you to follow the full route of this walk largely going downstream.

Most walks in the book are accessible by public transport so walks are not only accessible to car owners but for many who prefer public transport. Information about transport is given but you are advised to check current information as services vary from year to year. (See page 152)

The area of the book is one of fine, contrasting landscapes from moorland down to the coast, across undulating farmland and flat mosslands. Each landscape has a history to tell. The excellent work of Wyre Borough Council's Countryside Service and Lancashire County Council's Forest of Bowland Countryside teams and others have vastly improved the ease of use of much of the footpath network used in this book.

Many stiles are in better condition than when we produced the fourth edition. These people deserve our thanks for their achievements. If, however, you find a problem with a right of way described in this book do let Lancashire County Council know.

All distances given for each walk are approximate and we have included at the end of each paragraph a rough estimate of the distance covered in the route description in that paragraph. All sketch maps are very approximate and you will gain more enjoyment and accuracy of route finding by using the appropriate Ordnance Survey 1:25,000 Explorer Maps – two maps cover the walks in this book. They are OL 41 – Forest of Bowland & Ribblesdale, and 296 – Lancaster, Morecambe & Fleetwood.

When revising this book we have had some superb sightings of wildlife in the area – not least butterflies (one walk we encountered some 200 of about ten different species) and dragonflies (some ten or so different types might be encountered in summer). There are some fascinating wild flowers not least the so-called arable 'weeds' in the more intensively farmed areas. These include species which are nationally much rarer than they once used to be. Birds and mammals have also featured in the walks.

There are some fascinating historical sites to be seen on most walks and some of the more traditional vernacular farm buildings have date stones indicating when they might have been built.

We hope that users of this volume will enjoy the walks as much as we do when exploring this delightful area. Please remember the Country Code and have respect for the countryside and those who live and work there. We are grateful for those readers who have commented on previous editions and we hope that this one matches your aspirations.

Ian and Krysia Brodie
Easter 2008

Walks from
the Wyre Way

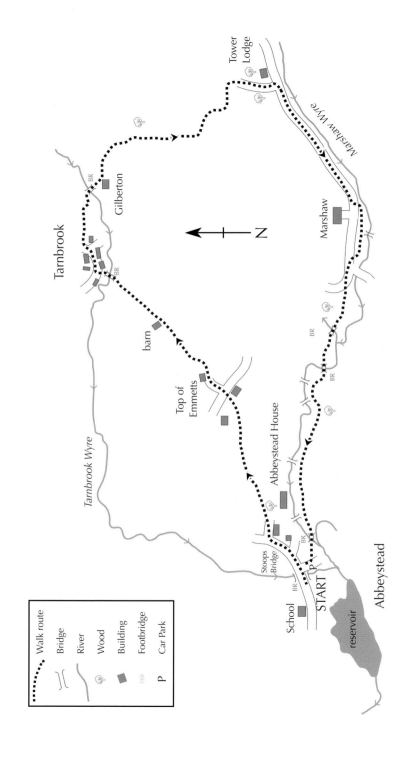

WALK 1

The Twin Rivers

Abbeystead – Tarnbrook – Marshaw – Abbeystead

LENGTH:	10 km (6 miles) Wyre Way: whole of walk
START:	Abbeystead hamlet by the school (GR 563543)
BUS:	Service 146 or 147 Lancaster to Abbeystead
PARKING:	Stoops Bridge, to the east of the school by the riverside
MAP:	O.S. Explorer OL41 – The Forest of Bowland & Ribblesdale

ℹ The whole walk forms the upper loop of the Wyre Way.

ℹ The River Wyre rises on the fells above Abbeystead and it is formed from two main tributaries, the Marshaw and the Tarnbrook Wyres. This walk explores the dales of these two tributaries. The whole catchment is owned by the Duke of Westminster and is managed for shooting and agriculture. The moors were once said to be the most productive grouse shoot in England whilst the copse-speckled landscape is designed for pheasant and rough shooting. This walks traverses an interesting mixture of landscape types.

ℹ Abbeystead House and its well cared for gardens are seen from the walk near the end of the route. The area was a medieval hunting chase – a claim that might still ring true. Also on the route, in various stages of decay are three privies and, especially around Ouzel Thorn, some good example of management of landscape features.

(🚶) **From Stoops Bridge, over the Tarnbrook Wyre, walk away from the hamlet pass the entrance lodge to Abbeystead House and then climb steeply uphill on the road. When the road bends left leave it to the right through the gate adjacent to the cottage and go to enter a field by the stile at the rear of the garage and garden. (600 metres)**

Follow the right-hand wall and deer fence but when it starts to curve away to the right cross the remainder of the field by going under the overhead power lines and aiming for the farm buildings ahead. Go over the stile by the right of two gates, just past the hare marker post. These carved stones are a superb contribution by local people to the character of Over Wyresdale parish. In this second field follow along the left hand fence to go through the kissing-gate by the gate in the far left-hand field corner. Cross the next field to reach the road by a stile found to the left of the gate-house cottage seen ahead. (900 metres)

Cross the road, go down the short access track to Top of Emmetts but just short of the yard turn right, over a stile and follow the left-hand boundary, and then cross the stile in the far left-hand corner of the field. In the next field follow the right-hand boundary and, after a short distance, cross the stile to your right, immediately followed by a second stile and plank footbridge. (300 metres)

(ℹ️) From the stile views of the amphitheatre of the Tarnbrook Wyre can be seen lying below the slopes of Ward's Stone Fell. To the south is the ridge of Haythornthwaite Fell.

(🚶) **In the field cross towards the lower of two barns, whose roof could be seen from the stile. On your way pick up** a left-hand fence line by the lapwing stone waymarker, and cross the next stile, footbridge and immediately adjacent stile, further down the left-hand fence. Go past the right-hand side of the barn and to meet the right-hand fence by the hat stone, then follow the right-hand fence to cross a stone stile in the far right hand corner. In the next field follow the right hand wall and fence, cross through the gated gap stile in the field corner, bear slightly left to cross the track and then a further gated gap stile. (1000 metres)

Cross the middle of the next field to go over a stile in the short section of stone wall and then directly across the field to climb the stile facing you. Go down the field to cross the stile by the gate at the bottom of the field and then cross the gated bridge over the Tarnbrook Wyre. Follow the short, enclosed track to the hamlet of Tarnbrook. Turn right to go through the settlement. (380 metres)

ⓘ The houses of the hamlet are of interest because of their vernacular features. The settlement is a 'closed' village in the Abbeystead estate but at one time it comprised 25 dwellings, of which nine housed Quaker families, and employed the skills of a hundred hatters and glovemakers. Tarnbrook was a vaccary (a farm site, see vaccary information box on page 111).

(🚶) At the far end of the hamlet go through the gate on the left at the end of the metalled road. Continue along this farm and moorland access track, bear right at the fork to go over the cattle grid and continue to pass a second cattle grid just short of Gilberton Farm and the river. (750 metres)

From the cattle grid go left immediately and cross the river by the footbridge upstream from the farm bridge. Continue ahead behind the farm and turn left on a track

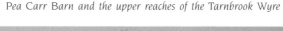

with a wall on your right. This track takes you over two small arched bridges, and through two gates to reach a yard between two barns. Bear right in the yard to leave by the first gate. (300 metres)

Turn left in the field and follow the left-hand wall up and then go through the gate in the top left-hand field corner. Continue upwards in the next field going parallel to the left-hand boundary and wood and cross the stile in the top left-hand field corner. Continue up in the third field and go through the prominent gate in the facing boundary. (375 metres)

Continue near the left-hand boundary, ignore the first, wooden, ladder stile but cross the next, iron, ladder

Pea Carr Barn and the upper reaches of the Tarnbrook Wyre

Grit Fell above Abbeystead

stile by the gate. You are now at the highest point of
the walk and on the edge of the moor. Here fields can
easily revert to moorland vegetation or, with drainage
and fertiliser, become grassy fields. Such is the dynamics
of the landscape. Go half-right to cross the next, shorter,
ladder stile and then half-left to cross the stone stepped
stile in the wall (an excellent example of 1990s walling).
Ahead of you is the view towards the road and the
melt-water channel that gives rise to the name Trough of
Bowland. (500 metres)

Go diagonally down hill to the far right-hand corner of
the field, passing concrete bases of war-time army huts.

Go through the gate, between the two wood corners, in the far right-hand field corner. Follow the track down to reach the road just beyond the gate at Tower Lodge. (375 metres)

Go right and follow the roadside until a cattle grid crosses it. (1500 metres)

On the left-hand side of the cattle grid go over the stile and follow the right-hand wall down the riverside field. Cross a small slab footbridge before crossing a further stile. Continue near the right hand wall to cross a further stile, by a footbridge, and then in the next field, follow the right hand boundary but, after 30 metres of fence beyond the walled section, cross the stile to gain access to the road-side. (500 metres)

Go left on the road, ignore the left turn (to Scorton) and continue until the road bends sharp right. Enter the field directly ahead by the stile and gate and follow the left-hand boundary along until the wall bends away to the left. From here go straight ahead and then down close to the right-hand wood to cross a footbridge with the river still to your left. From here to the start are a number of footbridges across the Marshaw Wyre but many are marked private and are not used on the walk. Pass through the subsequent gate and then follow the path by the left-hand fence until you have to cross a stile. Continue ahead to climb the hillock and then descend steeply to a kissing-gate and footbridge facing you. Cross the river here. (750 metres)

Go forward in the field to pass a sycamore and then climb gently to a lone holly tree. Now parallel to the river, on your right, keep your height above the river and below a wood above you to the left. The path gets nearer the river and then crosses a relatively level, grassy area. The river then meanders left toward a steep bluff. On the left is a flight of stone steps that lead you up the steep embankment to a stile and beyond you enter a short section of woodland. A stone commemorates a planting, in 1908, of the wood during the ownership of the Lord Sefton. Leave the wood by the kissing gate. (400 metres)

Keep near to, but above, the right-hand fence and parallel to the river as you traverse this long field. You pass the front of Abbeystead House and then gently descend to cross a footbridge near the end of this long field. (800 metres)

🛈 Abbeystead House was built in 1886 by the Earl of Sefton and is Elizabethan in style. The windows have mullions and transoms and it cost £100,000 to build. It is what one wag calls 'a palatial shooting box'.

Ⓧ **In the field follow the left-hand fence and then pass through the metal field gate before bearing right to reach the metalled road and your start at Stoops Bridge. (500 metres)**

NORSE NAMES – a number of the local place names appear to have a Norse origin. Those ending in fell (a hill), dale (valley) being the most obvious. Others include tarn (small lake), beck (stream), clough (or cleugh – a ravine), and Brock (brocc – a badger). Grizedale is the valley of the wild pig (griss). Hazelhurst Fell is the hazel wooded hillside (hyrst). Snape Rake Lane is the track up the hillside (from reik).

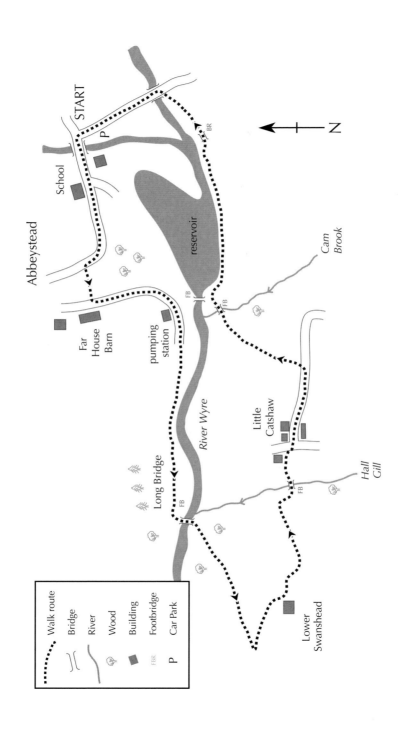

WALK 2

Upper Wyresdale: once the home of abbots

Abbeystead – Lower Swainshead – Catshaw – Abbeystead Reservoir – Abbeystead

LENGTH:	6.5 km (4 miles) Wyre Way: 2.6 km (and round reservoir loop) are covered
START:	Stoops Bridge, Abbeystead (GR 563543)
BUS:	Service 146 or 147 Lancaster to Abbeystead
PARKING:	Stoops Bridge, to the east of the school by the riverside
MAP:	O.S. Explorer OL41 – Forest of Bowland & Ribblesdale

ⓘ An excellent walk downstream of Abbeystead that reflects the nature of the young River Wyre. Steep wooded bluffs, riverside fields, and dramatic wooded clough streams tumbling down to the river. This walk, and Walk 16, pass a number of the interesting locally sculpted way-mark stones. For those interested in wildlife the reservoir adds a further dimension, the architecture of the reservoir provides another focus of interest.

🚶 **From Stoops Bridge walk through the hamlet of Abbeystead on the road to Lancaster, with the Village Hall on your left and the school on your right. Walk past** the telephone box and climb the hill with views of the reservoir down to your left. As the hill eases the road bends right by a house cross the stile by footpath sign on your left. Cross the field towards the left-hand building and pass through the obvious gate facing you to reach the concrete road beyond. Turn left down the road to pass over two cattle grids. (750 metres)

Just after the second cattle grid, and directly opposite the reservoir dam, the road meanders right but your route is to follow the left-hand wall down to re-meet the road near the stone faces of underground buildings. Rejoin the road and follow it past the structures with the River Wyre down to your left and, when the road bends left, continue ahead on a track to pass through a gate. (500 metres)

ⓘ The stone structures are part of the water supplies –water is piped here from the River Lune. This is the scene of the 1984 tragedy when a methane explosion killed a number of visitors and staff.

🚶 In the next, long, field follow the track ahead but, when the track bends to the right, continue straight ahead on slightly raised ground but parallel to the river. The path then goes alongside the left-hand fence passing a carved waymark stone (a fish). When the river bends away from the left-hand fence go diagonally up the slightly higher ground and parallel to the right-hand wood, pass a further stone (a duck), and then continue following the river downstream towards the end of the narrowing field. Just before the field ends the substantial wooden Long Bridge enables you to cross the River Wyre. (550 metres)

Turn right from the bridge and continue to the right, and initially by the riverbank, from the path junction. The clear path goes through Mark Holme Wood before climbing diagonally up the wooded bluff and away from the river. After the section of 'duck-boards' ignore the first stile and then a gate to your left but leave the wood by the second stile to enter a field. Contour ahead in the field, with Lower Swainshead Farm up to your left, but when a lone barn comes into view walk towards this to find a stile to cross the fence ahead, and then continue in the same direction to a meet the nearside of a stile by a gate. (800 metres) The Wyre Way continues from here in Walk 3.

To return to Abbeystead put your back to the nearside of this gate and stile and go diagonally right up the field and towards the left-hand side of Lower Swainshead Farm. Pass through a gateway, in the same fence that you have recently crossed by a stile, and then make to the right-hand boundary. Turn right to go through the gate in the right-hand wall to enter the edge of the farmyard. Then turn left and leave the track at the edge of the yard and go through the left-hand gate. Go into the long field and make towards the right-hand fence to meet a stile just beyond the right-hand gate towards the top right-hand corner of the field. Cross the stile and continue up the next field in the direction of Haythornthwaite Fell until you pass over the reedy ditch and the remains of an earthen bank, formerly a hedge line. From here bear slightly to your left and cross over the remainder of the field towards some trees with farm buildings showing behind the trees. This leads you to a stile that remains unseen until you are nearly there and which you cross the fence to enter the wood. (750 metres)

Follow the path diagonally right down the wooded clough and cross the wooden footbridge (built over a sadly semi-derelict packhorse bridge) over Hall Gill. Climb to the left to follow the path to a stile and then cross the stile to your immediate left. In the field turn right and go up by the unsightly storage tank and continue to cross the stile to the left of the pole mounted electricity transformer and gain the farm access road. (300 metres)

Turn right onto the road but immediately left at the junction to reach the yard of Catshaw Farm. (Little Catshaw on the map). Note the painted sign and the interesting ornamental gate. Continue along the track through the gated yard and on the track in the field beyond. Continue on this track until, after the field has widended on your right and shortly before the track bends to the right, you come to a right-hand waymark stone (a ram's head) on your right. Leave the track here by turning left into the field and follow the discontinuous line of hawthorns, a former hedge line, to reach a gate by the wood corner. Through the gate descend the next field sharply, initially by the right-hand fence, to go down to cross a footbridge over Cam Clough near where it joins the River Wyre. The path then goes along the riverbank to the side of an iron footbridge over the river. (1100 metres)

Wayside carving

Spillway at Abbeystead Reservoir

ⓘ Our way does not cross the river, however those with
time to explore may wish to cross the bridge and explore
the area around the dam to Abbeystead Reservoir with its
fish pass ladder, the grotto-like draw well and the superb
spillway where overflowing water makes a delightful sound.

🚶 **From the near-side of the bridge follow the stream
up, with superb views of the dam engineering, by the
spillway. The path now keeps between the reservoir
and the boundary wall. Later these features give way
to a wire fence and the wet areas near the river. The
clear, but sometimes wet, path leads all the way to the
road. Go left on the road to reach Stoops Bridge at
Abbeystead. (1500 metres)**

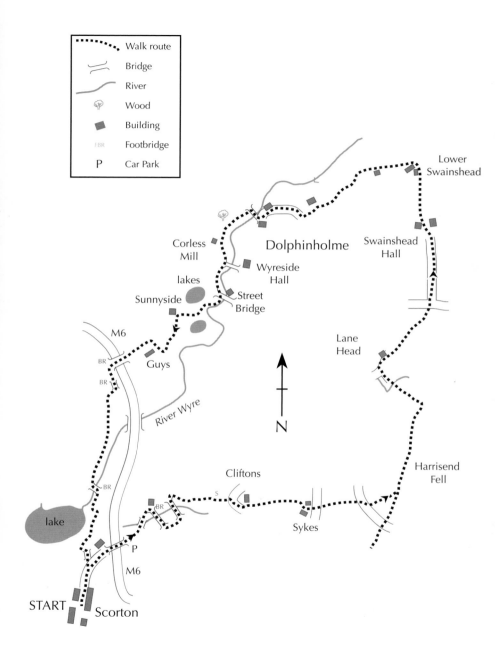

Walk route

Bridge

River

Wood

Building

FBR Footbridge

P Car Park

Lower
Swainshead

Corless
Mill

Dolphinholme

Swainshead
Hall

Wyreside
Hall

lakes

Sunnyside

Street
Bridge

M6

BR

BR

Guys

River Wyre

Lane
Head

N

Cliftons

Harrisend
Fell

S

BR

Sykes

lake

P

M6

START

Scorton

WALK 3

Nether Wyresdale: by fell and dale

Scorton – Harrisend Fell – Dolphinholme – Scorton

LENGTH:	16 km (10 miles) Wyre Way: 7.6 km
START:	Scorton Village centre
BUS:	Service 213 Garstang to Scorton or Services 146 and 147 Lancaster to Dolphinholme and Abbeystead
PARKING:	Centre of the village but this can be congested. There is limited space, on the route, just north of the bridge over the M6 (GR 505494).
MAP:	O.S. Explorer OL41 – Forest of Bowland & Ribblesdale

ⓘ This walk explores both the moorland edge and the middle Wyre valley. It is a walk of contrasts – fields, woods and moorland as well as the riverbank – and deserves a clear day to enjoy the views. The contrast between the river of the dipper, the rich field pattern of the oystercatcher, lapwing and curlew and the open fell of meadow pipit and grouse all contribute to the delights of the walk.

🚶 **Leave Scorton village centre and walk along the road signed to the Trough of Bowland and leave the houses behind. Continue over the motorway bridge and along**

Abbeystead Reservoir and its setting

until the road descends, bends sharp left and crosses a
stream. After another 40 metres leave the road by the
stile on the right (footpath sign Harris End Fell Road)
and then go ahead to cross the stream by the footbridge
under the huge spread of a beech tree. Follow upstream,
with the fence of the wood on your right, and re-cross
the stream at the next footbridge. (1.2 km)

Bear right after the footbridge and continue near the
stream, to cross the first of a series of stiles, in the fence
across your way. Go directly ahead to cross two fields
by two further stiles with the stream now down to your

right. A third stile to cross has taken you away from the stream. In the next field bear half-right to meet the far boundary opposite a small group of houses on your left, and which is followed to your right to leave this field by a stile near a gate in the far left-hand field corner. This leads to a road which you cross diagonally right and again enter a field by a further stile. Go directly up the field to cross a stile to the left of Cliftons Farm buildings. Turn right and follow the gated track into the farmyard and to the front of the farmhouse. (750 metres)

With the farmhouse on your left go through the field gate, go up the field by the left-hand fence and then cross the stile by the gate facing you just out from the left-hand field corner. Go directly ahead up a small rise to pass to the right of a dead oak tree. From this rise in the field there are extensive views of Morecambe Bay, the Lakeland fells and the area of your walk. Descend the rise aiming for the left-hand side of the farm buildings and cross the stile to the right of the junction of field boundaries ahead. In the next field follow near the left-hand boundary and enter the farmyard of Sykes Farm by the gate between the two outer buildings. (A permissive bypass path goes around the left of the farmyard.) Go right through the yard and left past the house to reach a road. (900 metres)

Cross the road directly to cross a stile and in the field go left of straight ahead to cross a stile in the fence across your way. Follow up by the left-hand fence in the next field and leave by the gate facing you in the boundary ahead. Go up the next field parallel to the right-hand boundary and pass through the gate in the highest part of the field. Just beyond is a further gate with a stile that takes you onto rougher, fell open access land. Go half right and keep above the banks of the stream down to your left to reach Harris End fell road by the footpath sign. (800 metres)

Cross the road directly and cross the rough ground until, about 100 metres directly above the road, you meet an obvious footpath. To avoid the rough ground you can go right along the road until a crest is reached where the same footpaths crosses the road. Your way lies to the left and follow the way-marked and generally distinct path across the fell side shoulder. This path is followed left over the moorland edge where views of upper Wyresdale open up, and then you meet a fence corner by a footpath junction. (1.9 km)

Turn left at this corner and go down the open fell land with the fence on your right. Cross the stile in the bottom right-hand corner and then go ahead down in the same direction near the right-hand boundary on what was an old lane, cross the small stream, and continue down the track to a track junction. Go right, through the gate, pass the derelict (it may be re-inhabited by the time you undertake the walk) Lane Head Farm. Continue along the line of the old track, through a gate and along the remains of the old enclosed lane, over a stream, until you bear right up a sunken lane to a gate and a derelict farmhouse with a privy. The track continues directly ahead, once hedged on both sides, begins to bend left, goes down to cross a stream, gently climbs to a gate, beyond which you go near the right-hand boundary through the further gate to arrive at a road. (800 metres)

Cross the road directly and go down the surfaced Waste Lane to the yard of Swainshead Hall Farm. Pass through the gated yard to the right of the buildings and continue down on the distinct track over a cattle-grid, at the left-hand of two gates, to reach Lower Swainshead Farm. When the track goes left into the yard just beyond the house go through the gate in the wall ahead. Turn left in the field, pass through a gateway in the fence below the farm and descend slightly across the next field to reach a gate and stile, hidden until you are close, across your way. (2.0 km) From here back to Scorton you follow the Wyre Way.

Go over the stile by the gate and cross the field towards the right-hand side of the stone barn ahead. Go to cross the stile by the gate in the right-hand field corner and behind the barn. Follow the short section of right-hand wall, and where it ends, bear left aiming for Dolphinhome Village, and contour through the field to cross a further stile by a gate. Follow the left-hand fence down this long field and pass through a gate in the far left-hand corner. Take the track ahead and go down the field to the gate in the lower right-hand corner of the field and above Dolphinholme House Farm. Continue down on the track and, still above the house, go left at the track junction. Follow the concrete, short farm access track to the road. Turn right on the road which leads down to the bridge over the River Wyre in Lower Dolphinholme. (2.0 km)

❶ On the building on the left before the bridge is a restored old gas lamp and reflects the fact Dolphinholme Mill, a worsted mill of 1787, was one of the first in the country to be illuminated by gas lights. It employed a thousand spinners and wool was combed in houses. The mill warehouse (1797), just over the bridge is now a terrace of houses.

🚶 Cross the bridge and just above the houses turn left off the road and take the lower of two paths to pass the sewage treatment plant and continue along a path with the wood on your right and, shortly, a wall on your left. Follow this path for its full length, pass through the small gate across your way and then cross the field aiming for the left-hand side of the group of trees and the farmhouse. Go into the farmyard by the small gate adjacent to the left-hand side of the house with the former water wheel of Corless Mill also on your left. This old corn mill displays the seventeen foot diameter, five foot wide waterwheel, two millstones and at Keepers Cottage a curious shaped roof. (800 metres)

Go along the farm access track, past the cottage and climb up the track with the river down to your left. As the track climbs and bends to the right go through a small gateway on your left. This leads you along a path above the river, through a small wood, and then by a small gate into the field. Follow the riverbank path down, pass the bridge to Wyreside Hall, and continue along the riverbank for about 60 metres to where the field is at it narrowest. Turn right to reach the road by a stile. The bridge gave access to Wyreside Hall. The house, dated 1852, with its dark grey stone, giant pilaster and porch of fluted ionic columns is well sited to enjoy views of the river valley. Turn left on the road (take great care) and then turn right to cross the stile at the near end of Street Bridge. (550 metres) Some people, rather than cut to the stile, continue along the riverbank to Street Bridge and access the road directly opposite the next footpath.

From this stile the path continues above the riverbank through a wood, passes a redundant ladder stile on your right and eventually leads you onto a track at the end of a fishing lake. Go left on the track, ignore the turn off to the left, and then follow the track right to reach, through the car park, the nearside of the house, Sunnyside. This area is a major tourism business and many tents and caravans may be found in this area of the walk. At the garden wall turn left to pass through the gate by the children's playground, and go half-right in the field cross a ladder stile by a gate (just beyond the caravan hard standing area) in the right-hand boundary. Turn left in this next field and follow the ditch along until the hedgerow crosses to your side of the ditch bank. From here cross the remainder of the field towards the left-hand side of the buildings ahead where there is a stile you cross situated half-way along the field boundary facing you. This is Guys and is a Girl Guide camp. After this last stile near the buildings, go down the left-hand side of these buildings, under the archway and, at the end of the buildings, turn right onto the track that passes the front of the house. (1.2 km)

Shortly along this track, and when the track leads to some big gates by the industrialised site at Nan Kings, go to cross a stile immediately on the far corner of this left-hand track. Turn left in the field and aim directly to cross the footbridge over the motorway – you have to cross a stile and a small stream across your path before the bridge is reached. Over the M6 turn left and go down into the lower field where you cross the dyke by a bridge and then turn right to follow the dyke side and following fence to reach a gate and stile at the far end of the field. This area is often very muddy. Cross the stile and follow the distinct path, along and near the riverbank, to the road at Cleveley Bridge. (1.4 km)

Turn left over the bridge and then almost immediately right over a stile by a gate and signed as the Wyre Way. Follow this track until it climbs up a small embankment. Leave the track by crossing the stile on your left then almost immediately turning right over another stile. Follow this narrow path by the left-hand fence with the wood on your right and, at the far end of the wood, cross over the stile into a field but with the old mill race to your right. Follow the race along the field edge path, cross a stile and two small plank footbridges, and continue to cross the stile by a gate to the right and rear of a tin shed. Over the stile go ahead to cross the footbridge and then continue to the double small gates. Through these cross the stone arched bridge over the mill race, follow the enclosed path along and, after a further footbridge and short section of path you emerge on the road. Scorton is to the right. (1.7 km)

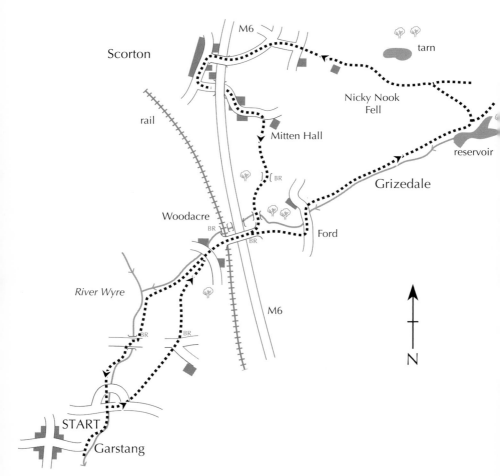

Scorton

M6

tarn

rail

Nicky Nook
Fell

reservoir

Mitten Hall

BR

Grizedale

Woodacre

BR

BR

Ford

River Wyre

BR

BR

M6

N

START

Garstang

WALK 4

Nicky Nook:
a perennial favourite

Garstang – Grizedale – Nicky Nook – Scorton
– Garstang

LENGTH:	11.5 km (7 miles) Wyre Way: 4 km from Scorton to Garstang
START:	Garstang Discovery Centre (GR 493454)
BUS:	Garstang is served by regular services from Lancaster, Preston and Blackpool (Services 40, 41, X42, and 42)
PARKING:	By Garstang Discovery Centre
MAP:	O.S. Explorer OL41 – Forest of Bowland & Ribblesdale

ⓘ This is the classic route for walkers from Garstang despite the need to use sections of country lanes. It encompasses the local fells, woodlands and water – elements which combine to make the Lancashire countryside so attractive. For a shorter variation of the walk of 8 km (5 miles) start at Scorton and omit the section from Garstang to the railway and M6 at Woodacre crossings.

🚶 **From the Discovery Centre go from the rear of the car park to the river and follow the path along the sports field-edge path and riverbank towards the bridge, and**

Grizedale Lea Reservoir

climb the steps up the near side of the bridge abutment. (400 metres)

ⓘ The bridge crosses the extraction point from the Lune-Wyre Conjunctive Use Scheme; from here water supplies are piped to the Frank Law Treatment works at Catterall before joining the North West supply grid. The upstream barriers are to prevent flood-waters from inundating villages down stream.

(⚐) Go over the bridge and just after the embankment track has joined from the left go left down steps to cross a stile and then across the field to a further stile. In the next field continue in the same direction to cross a further stile near the right-hand field corner. Go across the next field to meet the left-hand boundary, which is followed to a stile by a gate, and access to Wyre Lane. (500 metres)

Go right along the lane, bear left at the junction and immediately over the bridge go over the stile on your left. Cross the middle of the field to cross the footbridge in the facing hedge. Follow the right-hand fence in the next field, go over the stile in the far right-hand corner and continue along the fence line until it bends away to your right. (500 metres)

Bear right here and go through the kissing gate by a gate to the left of the wood. Keep near the stream but then go directly to pass through the gate in the section of stone wall at the far end of the field. Cross the road diagonally right and go down the short track to the left of the industrial buildings to reach the railway. (750 metres)

Cross the railway footbridge and subsequent motorway bridge and continue ahead to cross a stile by a gate by the right hand corner of a wood. Follow the track along with the wood on your left down to a stile and gate and the metalled lane beyond. Go left down the lane that crosses two streams, past the entrance to Throstle Nest houses on your left, and shortly, as the road starts to climb, a track signed as a bridlepath goes off to your right. (1.1 km)

Go down this track, through the gate and continue along the beck-side path to a further gate and stile (with a footbridge to your right). Go over the stile and continue along the obvious track as it climbs up the dale to arrive, after a further gate and kissing gate, at Grizedale reservoir. (1.7 km)

ⓘ Grizedale was damned in 1861–3. Whilst the waters are too acidic to be able to support much life it is not without its interests. Grizedale is Norse for the valley of the wild pigs. The valley contains many birch and oak trees and gives an indication of what the whole valley might have been like in more ancient times.

🚶 **Continue along the track until almost opposite the fork in the reservoir there is a break in the left-hand fence that gives access to stone steps and a stile in the wall with a footpath sign to Scorton and Nicky Nook. Cross the stile and climb the steep path that keeps near the right-hand fence and wall until, on the more gentle slope, a stile is seen in the right-hand wall. Do not cross but turn left and take the path that climbs gently to the triangulation point on the fell top at a height of 215 metres. (850 metres)**

ⓘ The fell offers extensive views of the Forest of Bowland moors, the Lakeland fells, the Fylde Plain and Morecambe Bay. On clear days the Isle of Man and North Wales can be seen. The spread of rhododendron and the state of some of the walls on parts of the fell cry out for attention.

🚶 **Leave the top by continuing along as if heading towards Morecambe Bay and the path leads down and right towards the pine trees above the topmost tarn. Keep to the left of these trees and from here the right-hand fence and wall lead down to a kissing gate above a small reservoir and then the path goes more steeply down to a stile to the right of a house at a road junction. Follow the road directly ahead all the way down to Scorton village. (2.0 km)**

ⓘ Scorton is an attractive village with the older properties built of the local gritstone. Refreshments and toilets are available but the village is often busy with tourists.

ⓧ From the bottom of Snowhill (the road you used to
enter the village) turn by the war memorial and school
and walk down the driveway to the church. Go through
the lychgate to the church grounds – the building of
1878–9 is a typical solid stone design of Paley and Austin
reflecting Victorian values, and cost £14,000 to build.
Just beyond the tower turn right through a small gate and
descend the field, past a huge oak tree, to a further gate
and the road. (270 metres)

Turn left on the road and, just after the bowling club,
left again into Tithebarn Lane. Go under the M6 and
continue on the road to pass a group of house on the
left-hand bend. After the last house on the right, East
Barn, go up the road to find a stile in the hedge above
the top of the garden. The footpath sign points us to
Hazelhead Lane. (550 metres)

In the field cross parallel to the M6 and pick up the
left-hand boundary that passes the house, Mitton Hall,
and leads to a gateway and stile in the far left-hand
corner. Now aim for the stile to the left of the corner
of the wood ahead. Over this stile follow the right-
hand fence of the wood to a footbridge and stile that
allows you to enter the wood. Turn left and follow the
track through the wood to a gate with a stile on its left.
(900 metres)

Cross the stile and go towards the right-hand corner of
the field and M6 to find a stile and then a path through
the gorse that goes over a footbridge. Zigzag up the
embankment, go over the motorway and railway bridges
and then ahead to the road. Cross the road and go
through the gate ahead with its Wyre Way footpath sign.
(300 metres)

Go down the field to pass through the kissing gate and
gate to the right of the wood and then follow the right-
hand stream down to the river Wyre. Turn left and climb
the slight rise of Broom Hill, a much eroded small glacial

Grizedale Beck

drumlin, and then descend to cross a stile and regain the riverbank path. Go along to pass the aqueduct and then go over the footbridge and to Wyre Lane. (1.0 km)

Cross the lane to a small gate, to enter Garstang Millennium Green, and follow the path along to a further gate by a wooden sculpture of a dipper. The surfaced path follows the riverbank via a stepped embankment and enables you to return easily to your starting point in Garstang. (1.0 km)

The name BOWLAND, or more correctly pronounced as BOLLAND, translates to the 'land of the cattle' – a reference to the urus, the wild cattle present in the wilder parts of Britain in pre-Roman days.

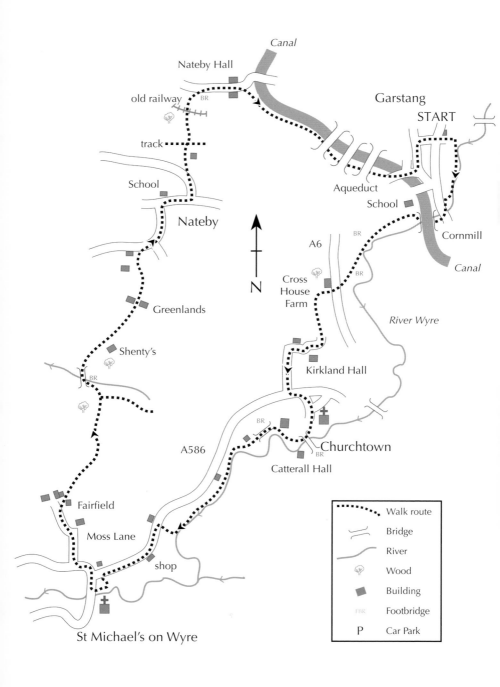

Canal

Nateby Hall

old railway

track

School

Nateby

Garstang
START

Aqueduct

School

Cornmill

Canal

A6

BR

BR

Cross
House
Farm

River Wyre

Greenlands

Shenty's

Kirkland Hall

BR

N

A586

BR

Churchtown

Catterall Hall

BR

Fairfield

Moss Lane

shop

St Michael's on Wyre

▪▪▪▪	Walk route
⌣	Bridge
—	River
🌳	Wood
▪	Building
FBR	Footbridge
P	Car Park

WALK 5

The Middle Reaches of the River

Garstang – Churchtown – St Michaels – Nateby – Garstang

LENGTH:	15.8 km (10 miles) Wyre Way: 6.4 km A shorter walk of 6.4 km can be made by following this route to St Michaels and returning by bus to Garstang.
START:	Garstang Discovery Centre (GR SD 493454)
BUS:	Service 42 Blackpool – Garstang – Lancaster links St Michaels and Churchtown
PARKING:	By Garstang Discovery Centre
MAP:	O.S. Explorer 296 – Lancaster, Morecambe & Fleetwood

ℹ This walk follows the Wyre Way downstream from Garstang to Churchtown and on to St Michael's-on-Wyre. If walkers want a circular route back to Garstang the walk suggested crosses the former mosslands on the Fylde and whilst few contour lines are crossed the fieldpaths can be wet after rainfall or, in summer, the long vegetation may slow the walker down. The route offers excellent views back to the fells of the Forest of Bowland and visits the interesting village of Churchtown.

🚶 Go down the side of the Garstang Discovery Centre, across the car park to reach the riverbank. Turn right and follow the River Wyre downstream on a tarmac path that eventually leads out on to the High Street. Turn left and cross the bridge over the river but then immediately cross the road and go down the short access to the Cornmill Nursing Home. (600 metres)

Pass under the archway of the building and go along the track that once followed the millrace and go to pass under the aqueduct by the riverbank. Climb the steps on the far side and reach the canal towpath. Cross over the aqueduct, the canal to your right, and walk along for some 80 metres until you find a gated stone-gap stile in the left-hand boundary. Here you are almost level with the Tithebarn canal basin. Leave the towpath through the small gate and cross the school field to pass through a kissing gate. (400 metres) The path is called Many Pads and was the main route to St. Helen's at Churchtown, once the Parish Church for Garstang.

Cross the next field to pass through the next kissing gate and then cross the field to find a stiled footbridge just up from the river bank besides a fenced area of land. The riverbank is now close to your left and this is followed until the river bends left. Look towards the farm buildings ahead and make directly for the third lamppost to the right-hand side of the tall farmhouse. Cross a further stiled footbridge and then climb the bank to reach the busy A6 road by a small gate. (500 metres)

Go left on the A6 verge but then carefully cross the road to arrive at the far end of the farm complex. Enter the concrete, gated farmtrack by the last house and continue along the track to follow alongside a wood until it meets two adjacent gates. Go left through the left-hand gate and follow the track along the left-hand field boundary until it bends left at the end of the field. Go through the gate facing you and then cross the next field

Churchtown

directly to a gate and stile in the far corner near the rear of Kirkland Hall. Beyond this is a track which you follow to the right, pass the rear of the Hall, Keepers' Cottage and Kirkland Hall Farm and then continue along the farm access road as it bends left to reach the main road just outside Churchtown. (1.8 km)

ⓘ Kirkland Hall has a seven-bay, two and a half storey brick façade built in 1760, but the rear wings contain some seventeenth century brickwork and date-stones from 1668 and 1695. The Butlers, whose home this once was, were adherents to the House of Stuart and when the King's forces captured Kirkland Hall they took Alexander Butler and his servant as prisoners, on horseback, to Preston. On the journey the servant slipped from his horse and unseated his master into a ditch. The troopers found him more dead than alive and left him to his fate. However he recovered, remounted and returned home.

Ⓚ Cross the A586 to the left and then go down Ainspool Lane, through the middle of the village, passing the market cross and the Punchbowl Inn to reach St Helen's Church. Continue through the car park and graveyard extension to reach a small gate by a seat. (500 metres)

ⓘ St Helen's claims the title of the 'Cathedral of the Fylde' and this large church is full of interest. Some of the stonework is twelfth century and the circular nature of the original churchyard suggests it was an earlier, pagan site. The interior has an elaborate carved pulpit of 1646, oak beams donated by Henry IV from his nearby Myerscough hunting chase, and rudely carved miserichords from Cockersand Abbey (see walk 14). The church tower is fifteenth century and the yard has some plague gravestones and two, with carvings showing people in prayer, are referred to as Adam and Eve. The river once lapped by the church and it has been suggested that the church owes its origin to Celtic missionaries who came up the river by coracle.

(*) **Follow the embankment towards the footbridge (built in 1985 to replace the suspension bridge washed away in 1980) and Catterall Hall, one of the oldest Wyreside houses, on the far bank. Do not cross the river but turn right to go downstream and cross a stile at the far end of the field. Continue along the bank-side path and follow the right-hand fence of the sewage works around to cross a footbridge over a tributary stream. Follow the right-hand hedge across the next field and then go to cross a stile in the boundary facing you. (600 metres)**

From now, until we rejoin the road, the path is a permissive footpath. Over the stile, with the river again directly to your left, continue to follow the right-hand fence (ignoring the right-hand stile) until a stile crosses your way. Over the stile follow the left-hand fence by the riverbank but half way down the field cross the stile on your left and continue now with the river still to your left but the fence to your right. Eventually the path goes around a short section of tributary stream, which it crosses by a bridge with a stile (the road lies just to your right) again goes left to follow the riverbank and then drops down to a stile on your right when a fence crosses your direct way along the riverbank. Cross this stile, go along the left-hand side of the narrow field and gain the road over a stile by a gate. Go left along the verge and then roadside footway into St. Michael's-on-Wyre, go past the shop, and The Oaks, then turn left down Allotment Lane. (1.8 km)

Follow this straight, short road until it goes left into a caravan site. Your way lies directly ahead through the gate. In a short distance and a small gate brings you to the riverbank and the path is followed to the right to

On the Lancaster Canal

reach the main road where it crosses the river to reach
the church. The Wyre Way continues ahead here but our
route back to Garstang turns right along the road to pass
the Grapes Inn. (300 metres)

ℹ️ The Grapes offers lunchtime refreshment on most days,
telephone 01995 679229, if you are walking out of the
main summer season to check.

🚶 Cross the main road from the Grapes and continue to
the road junction. Turn left down Rawcliffe Road, pass
Paddington Avenue but then cross the road to the right
and go down Moss Lane. This access road (cul-de-sac) is
followed all the way along until the surfaced lane ends at
Fairfield Farm. (1.3 km)

On approaching the farm pass the bungalow and first
of two buildings on your right and turn right on the track
between these two large farm buildings. The track bends
left to a gate by a squat tower structure. Go through the
gate, turn right on the track and through another gate
to enter a field. Leave the track here by turning right to
cross the field parallel to the obvious left-hand fence to
cross a stile in the patchy hedge facing you. Cross the
next field to go through the obvious gate directly ahead.

This leads to a track which you cross to a further stile
by a gate and enter another field. Follow the left-hand
hedge, cross the stile by the gate in the far left-hand
field corner, with a wood to the left, and then continue
along the left-hand boundary for the length of the next
field. In the far left-hand corner turn left to go through
the gateway with one stone stoop and then follow the
right-hand hedge until you are nearing the right-hand
field corner. Cross the stiled footbridge over Pilling Water
found on your right, some 30 metres short of the field
corner, and enter the next field. (1.0 km)

ⓘ These large, flat, regular shaped fields that once were
mossland give extensive views east to the hills of the Forest
of Bowland.

🏃 In this next field follow the left-hand hedge, pass through
the gate in the far left-hand corner and then continue
along by the left-hand boundary and go through the gate
facing you in the left-hand field corner at the rear of
Shentys Farm. Go directly ahead on the track that skirts
the left-hand side of the farm buildings. This then bends
to the right to meet the farm access track. Go left down
this track, ignore the left turn, and go straight to the
gate that leads to the yard of the former farm, now two
houses, at Greenlands. (1.0 km)
   Go through the gate, ignore the kissing gate to your
immediate right, continue straight ahead between the two
buildings and leave the enclosed area by a gate facing
you. Cross the small paddock directly ahead to cross a
stile and then cross the stile to your immediate right.
In this next field turn left to follow the long left-hand
boundary and go to cross the stile in the far left-hand
field corner. Continue along the left-hand boundary in
the next field and cross a further stile, on your left, in
the far left-hand field corner by a pond. Go right in this

next area to follow between the pond and a menage to cross a further stile. In the next field continue by the right-hand hedge and down to cross a stile in the far right-hand field corner. Go through the short woodland and gain the road by a further stile. (700 metres)

Turn right down the road and follow the main Garstang road passing the Baptist chapel and school, until, after leaving the far end of Nateby village, a road to Pilling, Kilcrash Lane, goes left. Go down this lane until it bends left. Cross the stile in the boundary facing you and then cross the field to pick up the right-hand boundary by the bungalow. Continue by the right-hand boundary and cross the stile in the far right-hand field corner, go right on the concrete road but shortly turn left over a stile into the field just before the gate over the track. (1.6 km)

ⓘ Beyond the farm is Bowers House, dated 1627, with a room once used as a Roman Catholic chapel or oratory. There were once unfounded rumours of a secret passage from here to Nateby Hall Farm.

⊛ Follow the right-hand field boundary and cross the stile ahead to continue on the path through the small wood and leave a by a further stile. Go to cross a concrete stile that once marked the line of the Pilling Pig railway line. Continue by the left-hand boundary down the next field but, when the boundary bends left after a clump of trees, cross the remainder of the field by aiming for a stile in line with the trees to the left of the farm buildings. Cross the stile and subsequent footbridge and then go right along the track to the yard of Nateby Hall Farm. The original hall was destroyed by fire in 1870. Go through the farmyard and, as the access track leaves and bends left, go to your right over the stile by the double gate into a triangular field. Go up the field towards the concrete blocks, pass between these and gain the canal towpath by a stile above the hidden and ruinous lime-kiln. The kiln once burned limestone brought down the canal from Kendal area for using on the local fields. **(1.3 km)**

To return to Garstang and your starting place go right along the canal towpath, pass the marina on your left, go under two road bridges, and then leave the canal by the next bridge. Go over the bridge and follow the road back to the centre of Garstang and to the Discovery Centre. **(2.5 km)**

VISITOR CENTRES
If you wish to acquire more information about the landscapes and wildlife you might see on the walks then Wyre Borough Council operates two centres. These are the Discovery Centre, High Street Garstang (01995 602125) and the Wyreside Ecology Centre at Stanah on the Wyre Estuary. (01253 857890). This last centre is visited on Walk 9.

USEFUL ADDRESSES
For footpath problems contact the footpath section of Lancashire County Council County Surveyors Dept, Guild House, Cross Street, Preston, PR1 8RD or via the LCC website.
For countryside matters contact the Lancashire Branch of the Council for the Protection of Rural England.
For wildlife matters contact the Lancashire Wildlife Trust, Cuerden Park Wildlife Centre, Bamber Bridge, Preston, PR5 6AU.
The Ramblers' Association Mid-Lancashire local contact is David Kelly, 4 Buttermere Close, Bamber Bridge, Preston, PR5 4RT.

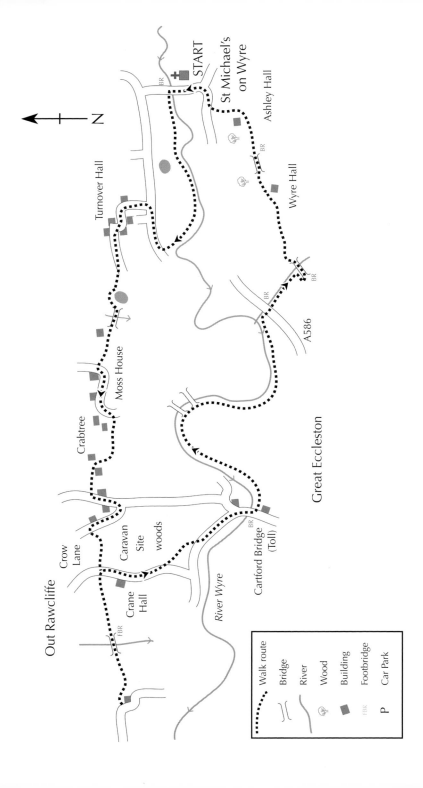

WALK 6

Where the River First Meets the Brine

St Michael's-on-Wyre – Out Rawcliffe – Great Eccleston – St Michaels

LENGTH:	12.3 km (7.75 miles) Wyre Way: 6.5 km
START:	St Michael's on Wyre Parish Church GR 462409
BUS:	Garstang to Poulton and Blackpool 42 & X42 Services
PARKING:	There is a car park just around from the Church in Hall Lane
MAP:	O.S. Explorer 296 – Lancaster, Morecambe & Fleetwood

ⓘ This walk uses a number of less frequented footpaths on the Fylde and a number of bird species can often be seen. Choose a quiet, sunny winter day with Cumulus clouds adding a skyscape to the open views and the fine landscape towards the Forest of Bowland. In early summer watch along the Wyre for the colourful banded demoiselle. The area gives you a perception of being wooded but the few small woods and the hedgerow trees are actually very thin on the ground.

ⓘ This section of the Wyre Way rarely sees the river however, more of the river –at its upper tidal limits, can be appreciated on our return route. St Michael's Church was said to have existed in 640 and was mentioned in the Domesday Survey of 1086. It was rebuilt in 1525 and the church is possibly a mixture of Thirteenth, Fifteenth and Sixteenth Century parts.

From St. Michael's Church cross the River Wyre by the footbridge and, on the far bank, turn immediately left, cross the road with care, and enter the riverside field by a kissing gate (Wyre Way sign to Rawcliffe Road). Follow the river along the embankment top, over a stile, pass the fishing ponds, across another stile and, after a further stile, a final stile gives access to Rawcliffe Road. Turn right along the road and turn into the second driveway on the left to Turnover Hall Farm. (1.5 km)

Go down the farm access road (Wyre Way sign to Lancaster Road) which bends left at the bungalow. Go straight into the farmyard (often very messy when wet, gated and thus not very rambler friendly) until a range of outbuildings blocks your way and with the house down to the left. Turn right here, go through the gate and then turn immediately left to pass the last buildings through a barrier type gate and continue directly ahead to leave the yard on a track. Ignore the track off to the right as you continue along a straight track that eventually leads into the right-hand of two fields. (650 metres)

Go along the field by the track along the left-hand boundary, pass the pond on your left, and continue in the same direction in the next field. Here you met a hard path which goes to the right, around a fishing pond, and after some 50–60 metres cross the stile to your right. Enter the field, go left and continue with the hedge on your left after rounding the field corner. Along this left-hand boundary you come to cross a stile by a gate. Turn right in the next field, to continue towards the tower silo of Wild Boar Farm, go over a stile by a gate but on a bridge, and then aim for the left hand of two gates in line with the building to the right of the silo. Wild Boar Farm lies to your right. Cross the stile by this gate, go diagonally left across the farm access track and then enter the field by a stile and gate with the silo on the immediate left. (650 metres)

Go directly ahead and leave this field by a stile and gate in the right-hand field corner by the side of the storage tank. In the next field cross directly towards the building to the right of the bungalow and cross two stiles in short succession to gain access to a farm road. Bear left and then follow the straight track, pass Fir Tree house and go to the track junction near the yard of Crabtree Farm. Cross the track, crossing your way, diagonally left to cross an obvious stile by a gate to re-enter a field. (700 metres)

Follow the right hand field boundary, pass the farmhouse, and then leave the field by crossing the stile facing you in the far right-hand field corner. Continue by the right-hand boundary in the next field and leave it by a further stile by a gate in the boundary facing you. Go diagonally right across the access track to a facing stile and gate, over which there is another stile immediately on your right which you cross into a 'garden'. Ignore the obvious signed stile ahead but go up the grassy area towards the right-hand corner of the house to cross a stile behind the large ash tree. Turn left on the track and follow this track past Bowland House and all the way along to a road. (1.0 km)

Go left on the road and, after some 100 metres, turn right into the gated Sandy Lane. (Wyre Way sign Crook Gate Lane) This track goes past Rowan Croft, and shortly after the semi-detached cottages comes to a gateway. Immediately through the gate turn left over the stile by the adjacent gate, go along a short enclosed green track to a stile and gate at the far end over which you enter a

Banded Demoiselle (female)

field. Cross the field to find a stile some 20 metres from
the left-hand field corner in the fence across your way.
In the next, narrower field cross almost directly to a stile
that gives you access to Crow Lane. (1.25 km)

The circular walk and the Wyre Way route part way
here. If you want to walk the whole Wyre Way then
follow the instructions in the next paragraph and return
to this point if you are to continue the circular walk.

🚶 Directly cross Crow Lane and the subsequent stile and
go down the field, initially by the left-hand fence, aiming
to the immediate left of the small wood ahead. Cross
the stile in the fence facing you and go down the next
field aiming for the white painted house to find a short
footbridge in the dip of the fields. In the next field follow

the right-hand hedge all the way to the gate in the top right-hand corner. Through this gate bear left immediately behind the house and reach the road through a gate. (900 metres) Go left down the road to the riverbank and the Wyre Way, the description of this route continues in Walk 7. To continue the circular walk turn left down the green track of Crow Lane and continue down the facing access track. Pass the caravan site, the ponds to your right and a wood on your left. Enter the field on your left by climbing the stile by the second gate on your left (opposite the start of a small wood to your right). Cross the field diagonally right towards a small triangular wood and enter and leave this wood by two consecutive stiles to emerge by the gateway to Rawcliffe Hall. Go right through the gate and to the road ahead where you go left on the road and follow the River Wyre along to the

Large Red Damsel

toll paying (pedestrians free) **Cartford Bridge. Cross the bridge. (1.6 km)**

Immediately over the bridge turn left on a track on the near side of the Cartford Hotel and go to follow the top of the riverside embankment. This leads over a stile by a gate, goes over a further stile by a gate to reach an aqueduct and adjacent footbridge (do not cross). Continue on the riverside embankment over three stiles by gates, two separate stiles and reach, by a further stile, the main A586 Great Eccleston – St Michael's Road where a small tributary drain joins the Wyre. (2.75 km)

❶ This section of the walk has great views towards the Bowland Fells, Beacon Fell and Longridge Fell. The village of Great Eccleston could be reached by any of the paths leading right from the embankment.

🚶 **Cross the road with care and then the facing stile. Go along the drain-side embankment until it is bridged. Cross the bridge and then walk diagonally left to cross a stile by an old gate where the left-hand hedge kinks. Follow the right-hand boundary and, after a stile by a gateway with stone gate posts, continue directly ahead aiming for the narrow but tall gate to the left of the buildings ahead. Through the gate cross the stile and gate immediate facing you. (800 metres)**

Go diagonally left to cross an access track to enter a field, which faces the front of the white painted Wyre Hall house, by the obvious stile. Walk by the right-hand boundary, cross the stile by the water trough and then go down this long field parallel to the left hand wood to cross the footbridge in the boundary facing you. Cross the next field, in the same direction to a stile, over which go left on the track for some 20–30 metres to meet a gate. Turn right in front of the gate, pass by the small, unfenced copse and then follow the left-hand ditch and

hedge along the left-hand edge of the field. Cross the stile in the far left-hand field corner and continue along the left-hand boundary to cross a further stile by the gate facing you. At the entrance gates to the grandly named Ashley Hall turn left down the lane to reach the main road and your starting point is to the right. (1.4 km)

THE WYRE WAY is the creation of Wyre Borough Council Countryside Service. They have two leaflets available on the route which, they suggest is a 66 km (41 mile) walking route and is covered in three sections. These are Fleetwood to Knott End at 26 km (16 miles) which are covered by our Walks 9 and 8; Shard Bridge to Garstang as 16 km (10 miles) covered by Walks 5,6 and 7; and Garstang to Tarnbrook/Marshaw as 24 km (15 miles) by our Walks 1, 2, 3 and 4. The routes in this book cover the route from the source down to the sea.

The Way has much to commend it with the river passing through differing landscapes and with a variety of wildlife –especially birds – to see. Copies of the leaflet can be obtained from Wyre Borough Council.

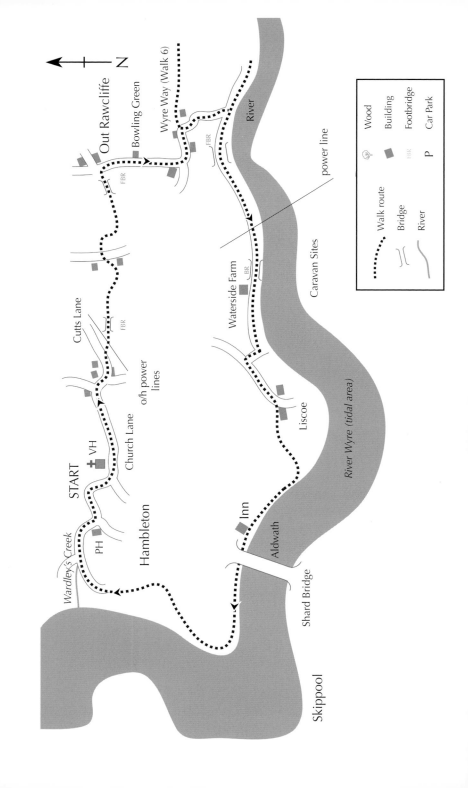

WALK 7

Down to the Saltings

Hambleton – Out Rawcliffe – Aldwath – Hambleton

LENGTH:	11.6 km (7 miles) – Wyre Way: 4.4 km
START:	Centre of Hambleton Village by The Shovels Public House (GR 371424)
BUS:	89 Lancaster to Poulton services to Hambleton – alight at The Shovels.
PARKING:	Politely in Hambleton
MAP:	O.S. Explorer 296 – Lancaster, Morecambe & Fleetwood

ⓘ This walk offers some pleasant stretches of the riverbank offering good sightings wildlife. However, the vegetation can be high in some places and walking can be hard and slow. Some country lane walking is involved and it visits an unusual pinfold. At high tide (9.4 metres and over or less when the river is in flood) some parts of this walk may be underwater.

🚶 **From The Shovels Public House go along the main road (Broadpool Lane) in the direction of Pilling, cross towards the small terrace of shops opposite the Police Station and then turn right, in front of Ryecroft Hall, into Carr Lane and its continuation, Sandy Lane. Walk the length of this road and turn left into Church Lane. Follow this**

past the Village Hall, School and Church until it meets
Ghants Lane at a junction. Turn right, and then almost
immediately left into Cutts Lane. (1.3 km)

Go along Cutts Lane, pass Moss Side Farm on your left
and, when under the over-head power lines, cross the
right-hand stile by the gate (with footpath sign) to enter
a field and to face a cluster of high voltage transmission
towers. Go left in the field, pass diagonally under the
high voltage overhead wires and then walk parallel to the
right-hand boundary to go to cross a footbridge in the
boundary facing you. Go along the next long field aiming
for the right-hand buildings to cross a stile almost at the
rear of a modern shed building where the field obviously
narrows. From the stile a short, enclosed path leads to a
further stile and the road. (900 metres)

Cross the road, diagonally to your left, and cross a
further stile. Follow the right hand boundary through
two short fields and bear right through the gate with a
stone gatepost in the far right-hand field corner. Walk
down the left-hand side of this narrow field but leave it
by crossing the footbridge and stile on your left part way
down the field. In the next field follow along by the left-
hand boundary, pass through the gate facing you in the
corner and, in the next field, follow near the right hand
boundary to cross a partially hidden stile (some 10 metres
from the old hedge field corner) in a temporary fence.
Continue in the same direction across the next short,
field to cross a footbridge and stile facing you. Continue
towards the white house by following near to the right-
hand field boundary to pass through a gate and reach the
road beyond. (700 metres)

Go right along the road to pass the restored pinfold
(with a welcome seat) claimed to be one of only six in
Lancashire, and continue, passing the bowling green,
through Out Rawcliffe to reach a road junction where
you go left along Whin Lane. Pass a number of houses

and, just short of Waters Reach house, you join the Wyre Way coming in from the left. (1.3 km)

Continue down the bending road until it bends left immediately above the riverbank. The next section is subject to tidal inundation and tall vegetation from late Spring. Leave the road to the right on the bank and go over the stile to follow the permissive path along the riverbank. Keep near the right-hand boundary and when you come to cross the footbridge you are back on a public right of way. Keep near the right-hand boundary until you rejoin the public right of way. Keep along by the right-hand boundary to a small footbridge and stile and then continue above the riverbank over a stile by a gate and then pass under the high voltage power lines. Continue by the right-hand boundary over two stiles in succession. After the second stile go slightly away from the right-hand boundary and, when facing the farmhouse at the far end of the complex to your right, go to cross a concrete slab bridge and towards the gates in front of Waterside Farm. (1.5 km)

Do not cross through by the gates but keep the farm and the boundary to your right and walk along an embankment (the farm access road is over the fence to your right). Cross the stile but, shortly after, the way is blocked by a fence. Leave the embankment by going over the right-hand stile by a gate and then follow the enclosed green lane away from the river. At the far end of this lane turn left to follow a farm access road (a permissive footpath) up to the front of Liscoe Farm. (1.4 km) The core of the farmhouse is probably an early Seventeenth Century construction.

Just beyond the farmhouse the track bends left into the farmyard. Continue directly ahead, through a gated track to keep all the farm buildings to your left and then enter the field. Follow the left-hand boundary down the long field, at one stage passing a pond on your right, to

The former Shard Toll Bridge

reach and pass through the gate in the boundary by the bottom corner of the field. In the next field continue ahead by the relic hedge-line but, just after half way along this boundary, go to cross the obvious gate (the second seen to your right) on top of the embankment. (600 metres)

Go right on the embankment, cross the stile and continue until the way is blocked by a hawthorn and there is a stile on your right. Do not cross this stile but drop down left to the saltings, then turn right to follow the path in tall vegetation along to pass the Shard Bridge Hotel and arrive under the right-hand arch of the new Shard Bridge. (900 metres) On your way you have passed the site of the old Shard Bridge which itself occupied the location of an ancient river crossing Aldwath (the old ford). Here we meet up with the Wyre Estuary Walk described in Walk 9.

Continue from under the bridge along the edge of the saltings to follow the River Wyre. The huge sweep of Skippool is best seen when the tide levels permit sailing to take place or when the tidal waters are ebbing or flowing. After the prominent right-hand gate of Bank Farm go along the embankment top towards the houses at Hambleton. Continue on the shoreward side of the

Common Hawker

Wyre evening

village to climb to and follow the surfaced track that
leads you to a road by Wardleys Creek (where the ferry
went to Cockle Hall and was the site of another historic
harbourage), and, beyond, the hotel. Some of the local
boulder clay deposits, besides the river, show rocks that
came from the Lake District in glaciers. Sea lavender
shows well its purple flowers here in June and July.
(2.5 km)

On reaching the road on near side of Wardley's Creek go to the right on the road (Kiln Lane) as it passes the houses of Hambleton, bends right and brings us back to the start at The Shovels. (300 metres)

ORDNANCE SURVEY MAPS: All the maps in this book are hand drawn sketches that are not to scale. They are to give some additional advice to the walker only. The authors believe that it is imperative that you carry and use the relevant Ordnance Survey Explorer Maps at the 1:25,000 scale. All the walks in this book are covered by two maps: O.S. Explorer Map OL41 – Forest of Bowland & Ribblesdale; and O.S. Explorer Map 296 – Lancaster, Morecambe & Fleetwood.

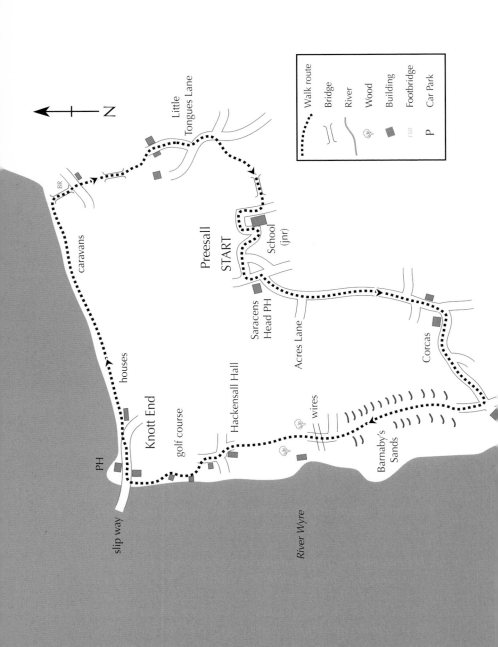

WALK 8

Amongst the Salt Mines

Preesall – Wyre estuary – Knott End – Preesall

LENGTH:	10.5 km (6 miles) Wyre Way: 3.5 km
START:	Centre of Preesall by Saracens Head Public House (GR 365473)
BUS:	Services 89 Lancaster to Poulton, or 2C Blackpool to Knott End
PARKING:	Politely in Preesall
MAP:	O.S. Explorer 296 – Lancaster, Morecambe & Fleetwood

ⓘ This walk explores the Wyre Estuary and the edge of Morecambe Bay. The route goes through the former brine fields and alongside a nature reserve the Wyre estuary. The last stages of the Wyre Way (the estuary loop covered in Walk 9) are described.

🚶 **From the south side of Preesall's Saracens Head Public House go down Back Lane, pass Acres Lane on the right and then, after some distance, Cemetery Lane on the left. Continue on Back Lane to pass semi-detached cottages, go over a bridged dyke and, shortly after, an untidy farm, Corcas, marks where you turn right and go down an enclosed track (marked private road and bridle path). Follow this past the farm and all the way until it meets the metalled road end by the collection of**

bungalows and caravans at The Heads. (2.7 km)
When you arrive at the Heads the Wyre Way comes
along the road from the left.

ⓘ On your way the lane has interesting hedgerows, provides
views of the stump of Preesall's windmill and, on more open
parts as it meanders amongst the drumlins, views east to the
Forest of Bowland where lie the headwaters of the Wyre.

ⓘ The area to the right of the embankment is the Preesall
saltfield that was re-discovered in 1872 during prospecting
for iron ore. The rock salt occurs in 120 metre thick beds
and is exceptionally hard – originally it was mined with
the help of blasting. The first sample of salt was produced
after the prospectors returned to their lodgings and their
landlady dissolved, filtered and evaporated the water to
produce the mineral.

A mine was opened and salt was taken by a small
railway along the track you have now reached to the
estuary side where it was shipped out to Australia, South
America, the Baltic countries, Canada, India, Burma, and
Iceland. The few remaining extraction points show where
water was used to dissolve the salt and the brine produced
pumped out. This left salt pillars between the wells and
avoided ground collapse that was once a major problem
but created the interesting ponds in the area.

Salt was known in the area earlier as some of the local
names reflect and there are records from the fifteenth to
the eighteenth century of the evaporation of sea water in
the locality.

🚶 **Turn right here, by the Wyre Way signpost and go along**
the short track to climb the stile and then walk the
length of the embankment beyond. Go straight ahead
along the embankment, ignoring paths off to the right,
and at the far end, after a stile, arrive at a track by a

footpath sign just short of some over-head power lines. (1.5 km)

ⓘ The saltmarsh to the left is Barnaby's Sands, a Site of Special Scientific Interest (SSSI), managed by the Lancashire Wildlife Trust. This SSSI is an ungrazed saltmarsh, which along with nearby Burrow's Marsh form a unique wildlife resource in the County. Although the nitrate and phosphate rich waters of the estuary have encouraged the invasion of cord grass (*Spartina*) since the 1940s the zonation of vegetation and the occurrence of some flowers such as the unique rock sea lavender make this a fascinating comparison with grazed saltmarshes. These areas also provide wader and wildfowl roosts and therefore walkers need to minimise any disturbance of roosting birds.

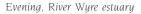

Evening, River Wyre estuary

Fleetwood and the River Wyre's mouth

From the end of the embankment go directly ahead on the track to pass under the several lines of overhead power wires, continue past two small windswept woods, over the lower reaches of the golf course and arrive at the track junction by the side of Hackensall Hall. (1 km)

The name of the Hall is derived from the Viking personal name Hakon who probably settled in the area in the ninth or early tenth century. The hall was built by Richard and Anne Fleetwood of Rossall in 1656 as their original house site was vulnerable to flooding. There may have been an earlier moated house on the site. During a nineteenth century renovation it is rumoured that two concealed skeletons were found in walls. There are stories of the house being haunted by a horse. A hoard of around 500 Roman Coins was found nearby in 1926.

Go left at the track junction, bending to keep all the buildings to your left, and then turn right to re-enter the golf course by some of their buildings. At the signpost continue over the golf course to head for the prominent overhead wire pole by a tin-shed. With the estuary

Fleetwood and the Wyre Estuary, from Knott End

and Fleetwood now below you to the left go along the edge of the course and bear left immediately after the cottage to reach the river-side embankment. Go along the embankment to the ferry slipway and the cafes and toilets of Knott End. (1 km)

ⓘ This is good place to watch the ships and the birds. One story says that the Norse marked the navigable channel of the river by cairns or knotts and the final one being Knott End. The railway, the terminal station now being the café near the golf club house, arrived in 1908. The ferry to Fleetwood operates seasonally. You have completed the Wyre Way.

Another view of Fleetwood and the Wyre Estuary from Knott End

(🚶) To continue the walk go along the road away from the slipway and just after the Bourne Arms follow the promenade along the shore of Morecambe Bay. Continue to the shoreward side of the houses and the path then follows the sea defence wall. After the last houses the wall passes Brookfield House caravan site and, almost in the next field, Sandy Bay caravan site. (1.95 km)

Leave the seawall by the right-hand steps immediately after the second of these caravan sites, descend to an enclosed path which is followed, with the caravans on your right and a dyke on your left to reach a road. Cross the road diagonally left and re-enter the fields by a stile alongside a gate adjacent to the house. For the next few fields keep by the right-hand dyke (Wheal Foot Watercourse). This is followed over four stiles, then a footbridge (near a footbridge to the bungalows on your right) and then by some further stiles by gates, to emerge by a gate, onto a track. Bear left on the track and this becomes Little Tongue's Lane as it passes an increasing number of houses to reach a main road by Preesall Garage. (1.5 km)

Turn left along the road, cross and then continue to a stile on your right by a bus stop sign on a lamppost and just after the white bungalow, Pennine View. Over the stile follow the enclosed path to cross a further stile. Go left to cross the next, obvious, stile in the fenced field corner and then bear right to go to cross the footbridge. Climb the steep slope ahead and go over the stile opposite the school grounds. Looking back the vista of the Bowland hills and the Fylde plain is worth a rest. Follow to the right the meandering enclosed path, around the school grounds, and from the school entrance go down School Lane to end your walk at the Saracens Head. (750 metres)

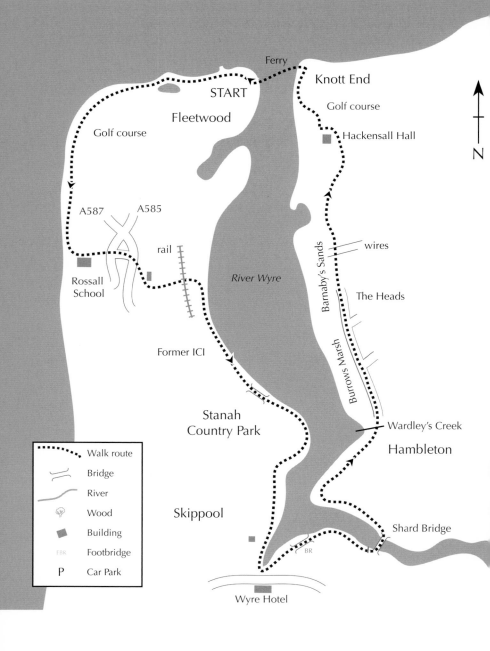

Ferry

Knott End

START

Golf course

Fleetwood

Hackensall Hall

Golf course

A587   A585

rail

River Wyre

Barnaby's Sands

wires

The Heads

Rossall
School

Former ICI

Burrows Marsh

Wardley's Creek

Stanah
Country Park

Hambleton

Skippool

Shard Bridge

BR

Wyre Hotel

N

Walk route

Bridge

River

Wood

Building

FBR   Footbridge

P   Car Park

WALK 9

The Wyre Estuary Walk

Fleetwood – Stanah – Hambleton – Knott End

LENGTH:	25 km (15 miles) – all Wyre Way
START:	Fleetwood Wyre Ferry Terminal (GR 341480)
BUS or TRAM:	To North Euston Hotel, Fleetwood (services from Blackpool, Lancaster (via Knott End), Poulton and Thornton Cleveleys
Should the Knott End to Fleetwood estuary ferry not be running then a bus can be used to return to the start.
PARKING:	In Fleetwood near the promenade, or in Knott End
MAP:	O.S. Explorer 296 – Lancaster, Morecambe & Fleetwood

ⓘ The whole of this walk is a loop of the Wyre Way around the estuary of the river.

This walk has much to commend it at all times of the year. At most times of the year the sea and the Wyre estuary provide interesting wildlife sightings and, in winter, the section along the sea defence wall can be dramatic during high tide with the waves rolling against the promenade. Some sections are impassable during very high tides and one short section, Skippool to Shard Bridge, is frequently very wet underfoot. On a clear day you can see three National Parks and three Areas of Outstanding

Natural Beauty. The section from Rossall to Fleetwod, along the sea wall, is shared with the Lancashire Coastal Path.

The mouth of the Wyre has long been regarded as a sheltered anchorage and was perhaps the Roman port called *Portus Setantiorum*. The mouth of the estuary is actually narrower than much of the estuary and, in much earlier geological times, the river may have reached the sea nearer Blackpool. This walk is a fine and fitting conclusion to a river that the Wyre Way has followed from source to sea.

☈ **From the ferry slipway, opposite the North Euston turn right to pass the RNLI lifeboat station and continue to pass the small lighthouse and then the diminutive pier. Just beyond the pier turn right to follow the track to the sea edge promenade. From here follow the roadway and then concrete sea defence wall all the way past the marine lake, around Rossall Point, past the golf course (where the route is paralleled by a footpath to the lee or shore side of the sea wall) and continue heading south towards Blackpool Tower. Eventually the high left hand wall becomes lower by a gate and lifebuoy and with the number G23 attached to the sea wall. Go left through the gap to leave the sea defence. (5.5 km)**

From the gap go down the ramp and through the adjacent gate. Follow the right hand fence through the field, with Rossall School to the right. After crossing through the small second field go through a further gate to follow the school access road ahead then round to the right and left to meet the main A587 road. Cross the road and tram track carefully and go down the facing Rossall Lane (B5409) to reach Amounderness Way (the A585). Cross this directly to go along a further cul-de-sac lane to the far end where it meets a larger road opposite a caravan site. (1.25 km)

ⓘ The name Rossall is thought to be derived from the
Celtic Rhos meaning moor. The Abbey of Dieulacres in
Staffordshire once owned the land around the school but
on dissolution it came into the hands of the Fleetwood
and Fleetwood-Hesketh family. The land was given to the
school in 1844 and was the site of Rossall Hall.

🚶 **Go right down this next road but cross over to the left-
hand pavement. Walk along to the end of the caravan
site (Carla Gran) and turn immediately left at the end
of a short terrace of houses. With the industrial site on
your right go towards a gate way and cross the stile to
its right and follow along the raised bank top path with
old hawthorns forming an avenue. At the end of the bank
cross the stile and the railway line. Go forward through a
gap between the high metal fences and the enclosed path
leads you to the river bank. (1.5 km)**

ⓘ The huge former industrial complex was originally the
Fleetwood Salt Company, later ICI, which processed
rock salt and brine from the salt field across the Wyre
and which will feature later on this walk. The brine was
pumped under the river.

🚶 **Turn right alongside the site fence with the estuary to
your left. When the track forks go left (the left-hand pipe
goes under the track) and continue along the riverbank
to a stile. Over the stile the path is above a caravan site
to your right and eventually leads, by a bridge over a
dyke flowing into the Wyre, to a car park and the Wyre
interpretative centre and Stanah Country Park. (2.5 km)**

ⓘ This area, well managed by Wyre Borough Council, has
a car park, picnic site and visitor centre by the estuary.
In the 1960s the saltmarsh was enclosed by embankment
and used as a council refuse tip but was reclaimed in the

1980s. The centre has an information point, exhibitions of the estuary's wildlife and heritage, small shop, refreshments and toilets and is well worthy of a visit.

⊛ **To continue the walk keep left, along by the estuary, and take the paths nearest to the river by the edge of the salt marsh. From here to Skippool, Shard Bridge and on to Wardleys the path may be flooded during very high tides. The surfaced path, (signed Cockle Hall and Skippool), clings to the side of the estuary as it passes the Cockle Hall picnic site goes round the bay called Ramper Pool, and then bends to pass a plethora of moored boats with their precarious timber walkways to reach the sailing club base. Go in front of the sailing club base, continue along the track and the road which follows the river and then Skippool Creek. When the hotel appears on your left leave the road on the creek-side footpath sign to the left and follow this towards a stile that, if climbed, would access the road almost opposite the tall River Wyre pub. (3.5 km)**

Do not cross the stile but go left over the culverted creek and then left again in the field with the creek still on your left. Follow the left-hand field edge then cross a bridge, over a further creek, climb the short path and, in the next field, follow the left-hand edge of the field towards the River Wyre. Continue on the field edge above the Wyre to reach a footpath sign and some steps in the far-left hand corner of the field. Descend the steps and, after the short boardwalk, follow the frequently very wet path near the right-hand edge of the salt marsh towards Shard Bridge. A track leads up the far embankment to a gate to reach the road over the bridge. Go left over the bridge to the far bank. (1.75 km)

ⓘ Edward III noted Skippool in 1330 when he granted a road from Poulton. The pool, through Main Dyke, drains

Pharos Lighthouse, Fleetwood

Blackpool's important nature reserve Marton Mere. Skippool was a harbour in the sixteenth and seventeenth century when wines, spirits, tea, tobacco, rum, sugar and timber were imported. The Shard Bridge was built in the 1990s to replace the toll bridge of 1864. The site is Aldwath one of the old fords of the Wyre – the name deriving from Old Norse.

(※) At the end of the bridge turn left and go past the gate down to the salt marsh. Go right, along the edge of the saltings to follow the river. By the prominent gate of Bank Farm go along the embankment top and continue on the shoreward side of the Hambleton village to pick up a surfaced track that leads you to a road. Turn left to reach Wardleys Creek (where the ferry went to Cockle Hall and was the site of another historic harbourage), and the hotel. Some of the local boulder clay deposits, besides the river, show rocks that came from the Lake District in glaciers. (2.25 km)

From here to the Heads the Wyre Way continues along narrow lanes, keeping left at any junctions, passing the hamlet of Staynall and Burrows Marsh (a Site of Special Scientific Interest). (3.25 km)

Turn right here, by the Wyre Way signpost and go along the short track to climb the stile and then walk the length of the embankment beyond. Go straight ahead along the embankment, ignoring paths off to the right, and at the far end, after a stile, arrive at a track by a footpath sign just short of some over-head power lines. (1.5 km)

ⓘ The saltmarsh to the left is Barnaby's Sands, a Site of Special Scientific Interest (SSSI), managed by the Lancashire Wildlife Trust. This SSSI is an ungrazed saltmarsh, which along with nearby Burrow's Marsh form a unique wildlife resource in the County. Although the nitrate and phosphate rich waters of the estuary have encouraged the invasion of cord grass (*Spartina*) since the 1940s the zonation of vegetation and the occurrence of some flowers such as the unique rock sea lavender make this a fascinating comparison with grazed saltmarshes. These areas also provide wader and wildfowl roosts and therefore walkers need to minimise any disturbance of roosting birds.

🚶 **From the end of the embankment go directly ahead on the track to pass under the several lines of overhead power wires, continue past two small windswept woods, over the lower reaches of the golf course and arrive at the track junction by the side of Hackensall Hall. (1 km)**

ℹ️ The name of the Hall is derived from the Viking personal name Hakon who probably settled in the area in the ninth or early tenth century. The hall was built by Richard and Anne Fleetwood of Rossall in 1656 as their original house site was vulnerable to flooding. There may have been an earlier moated house on the site. During a nineteenth century renovation it is rumoured that two concealed skeletons were found in walls. There are stories of the house being haunted by a horse. A hoard of around 500 Roman Coins was found nearby in 1926.

🚶 **Go left at the track junction, bending to keep all the buildings to your left, and then turn right to re-enter the golf course by some of their buildings. At the signpost continue over the golf course to head for the prominent overhead wire pole by a tin-shed. With the estuary and Fleetwood now below you to the left go along the edge of the course and bear left immediately after the cottage to reach the river-side embankment. Go along the embankment to the ferry slipway and the cafes and toilets of Knott End. (1 km) This is good place to watch the ships and the birds. One story says that the Norse marked the navigable channel of the river by cairns or knotts and the final one being Knott End. The railway, the terminal station now being the café near the golf club house, arrived in 1908. The ferry to Fleetwood operates seasonally. You have completed the Wyre Way.**

A ferry service should be running from Knott End to Fleetwood to return you to the start of your walk.

WOODLANDS: Lancashire has a very low percentage cover of woodlands and many regard the county as suitable for much more planting. Some of this future planting may be conifers but others may be native woodlands. Many of the walks in this book rely on woodlands for adding variety to the landscape and anyone who doesn't know the county and has only used these walks could be forgiven for thinking that the county is well wooded.

Despite the plethora of woodlands seen from these walks a few thoughts that may put them more in context. In the Fylde area the flat landscape looks well wooded due to the number of hedgerow trees that are seen. However many of these are old and not being replaced. In the Bowland foothills there are a mixture of woodlands. Some are maintained for pheasant rearing or form part of a rough shoot. Other rectangular block woodlands of conifers look strangely placed in a rounded landscape. The more deciduous woodlands, for example along the Brock, look at their best in autumn but many are poorly, if at all managed and are slowly losing their native character.

Sycamore and beech are common in the area yet these attractive trees are often growing at the expense of native species and so can be detrimental to wildlife. There is a case for restoring more of these woodlands as native woodlands that will have a more representative ground flora (see the bluebells during spring to see what we might be missing).

Other Walks from Garstang and the Surrounding Countryside

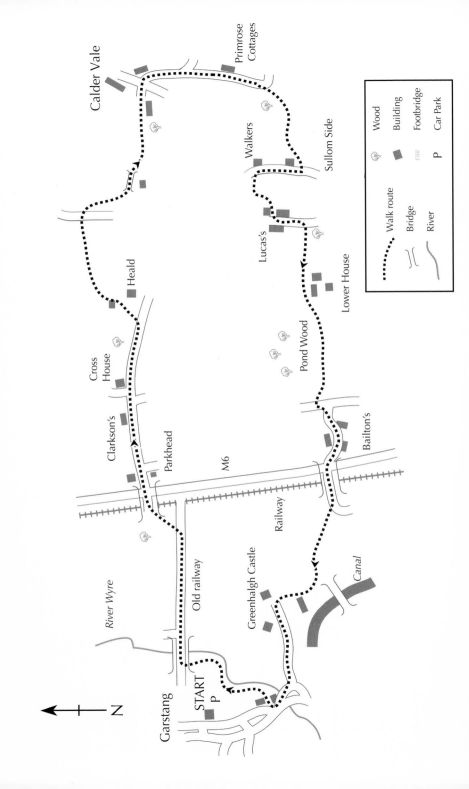

WALK 10

Mills on the Calder

Garstang – Calder Vale – Garstang

LENGTH:	8 km (5 miles)
START:	Garstang Discovery Centre (GR 493454)
BUS:	Garstang lies on the main Preston to Lancaster route (services 40, 41) and Lancaster to Blackpool route (services 42 and X42)
PARKING:	By Garstang Discovery Centre
MAP:	O.S. Explorer OL41 – Forest of Bowland & Ribblesdale

❶ A walk mostly over field paths and tracks that combines aspects of industrial archaeology with fine prospects of the landscape. In bluebell time the woods along the route can be spectacular but this walk is an all year round favourite because of the views across the Fylde plain to the coast and towards the moorlands of the Forest of Bowland.

Ⓧ **From the Discovery Centre go across the car park to the river and follow the paved path upstream, with the sports field on your left, to reach the embankment and bridge across the River Wyre. Go up the steps on the left near side and go over the bridge and continue to the stile facing you beyond the end of the tarmac track. (400 metres)**

ⓘ The bridge was formerly the crossing point of the old Garstang to Knott End railway known locally as the 'Pilling Pig'. It operated, largely unsuccessfully, between 1870 and 1963.

☈ **Continue along the enclosed path, the former line of the railway, down over a small stream, up to cross a stile and continue under the overhead power lines. Continue along the trackbed but, when it goes into a cutting, follow up the left-hand embankment to a stile by a set of steps. (600 metres)**

ⓘ The cutting took the railway to join the mainline at the former Garstang and Catterall Station but from the bottom of the steps forms a memorial nature reserve to which you have permissive access. In the cutting are smaller exposures of the underlying friable sandstone, a rock that serves as an aquifer.

Greehalgh (Garstang) Castle

Calder Wood

🚶 Over the stile go half right across the field, pass the corner of the wood aiming for the motorway bridge and then climb the stile by the gate in the far corner of the field. Turn right on the track to cross over the railway and the motorway, with a stream crossing on the bridge, to reach Parkhead. (300 metres)

Go straight up the gated metalled access track, ignoring any turns off to the right or left and eventually go to pass Clarkson's Farm on your left, and continue up to meet the road where it bends. Your way is directly across to the right of white painted Cross House and Cottage and up the track towards Heald Farm. (500 metres)

ℹ️ The houses are named after the site of a wailing cross, whose base stone is apparently now buried, where coffin bearers could rest and the mourners wail.

(🚶) The track climbs past a wood on your left and, just short of the buildings of Heald Farm, turn left over a stile into the bottom of the next, smaller wood. Go up the 'open' wood, near the left-hand fence, and leave it by the stile and gate in the top corner. Go left along the short track to cross a stile by a gate and corrugated iron barn and then go ahead into the field by another gateway by way of a small gate. Turn right and follow the right-hand boundary up to the top of the field, crossing any stiles that might be in place. (600 metres)

ⓘ This is the highest point of the walk and from where extensive views across the Fylde to the coast and the Lake District can be seen. Eastward lies the moors of the Forest of Bowland AONB.

(🚶) Go through the gap stile by the gate and continue down by the right-hand boundary using two further stiles by gates, (part of the boundary is a line of beech trees), to reach the road by a further stile and gate. Turn right and cross the road diagonally towards the gateway to 'The Paddocks' and, in front of the gate, go right along a short enclosed path and cross the stile at the end. Continue by the right-hand ditch and, over the stile in the corner, go left along a short enclosed path to cross a short footbridge and re-enter fields. Go directly across and pass through the gateway to the immediate right of the electricity pole and then cross the next field in the same direction to an obvious stile by the corner of the wood. (550 metres)
From here an enclosed path leads past a small wood, rear gardens of houses and down some steps to the road into Calder Vale. (200 metres) The centre of the village and the last working mill are down to the left.

ⓘ Calder Vale is a most unexpected site – an industrial stone built village enveloped in the fold of the Bowland hills. The

vernacular architecture is not without character. The mill
was built as a four-storey cotton mill in 1835 with thick
stone outer walls and cast-iron pillars. There are remains
of the former mill-race and mill-pond above the village.
The waterwheel was replaced by a turbine, later a beam
engine and, in 1909, a gas engine but is now electrically
driven. The mill and village were built for the Jacksons, a
Quaker family. The lack of a public house in the village
is due to the family not wishing to see 'ragged children'.
Brothers Richard and Jonathan founded the cotton mill
whilst brother John opened a paper mill upstream at
Oakenclough.

🚶 **From where you emerged on the road turn right down
Albert Terrace and follow along the track to the isolated
terrace of Primrose Cottages. (450 metres)**

ⓘ The track passes through steep-sided woodlands that are,
each Spring, carpeted in bluebells, passes above the lodge
of the other village mill and the rocky-bed of the River
Calder to reach the terrace formerly comprising twelve
mill-workers cottages and mill-owners house. The Barnace
Weaving Mill has been demolished but reservoir sites and
a mill-race can be seen from the walk. This mill, sited
beyond the cottages, opened in 1845 and was powered by
a waterwheel and, later, a steam engine whose chimney
was constructed up the hillside.

🚶 **Continue past the cottages and gate until the track bends
sharply left. Go right and climb the sloping path up
through the wood to re-enter a field by a gate. Follow
the left-hand fence to cross a stile by a gate in the far
left-hand field corner and then continue ahead and down
a rough track, by two further gates, to reach the road by
Sullom Side Farm. (650 metres) The farm sometimes sells
ice-creams.**

Follow the road to the right to reach the next building, Walker House. Cross the road to a gate and stile and re-enter a field. Go down the first field by the right-hand boundary, pass through a gate, and go diagonally left to aim for the farm-house and enter the rear of Lucas's Farm by a gate and stile. (550 metres)

Go down the right-hand side of the house, turn left on the farm access road and, after 20 metres, go through a small field gate on your right just prior to a small wood. Go down the wood edge, over a further stile and go down the longer field to a gate in the far bottom left-hand corner (hidden beyond the outbuildings of Lower House). (250 metres)

Cross through this gate, turn right, and go to a stile in the far right-hand corner of the field that lies opposite a pond in Janet's Hill Wood – a wood with a Eucalyptus tree planted in the 1990s as a memorial to a soldier who died in Burma in 1945. Continue along the right hand boundary to the corner of the wood (the tree is just to your right), cross the stile and go left across the field to cross a further stile by an obvious gate some 20 metres from the left-hand corner. (300 metres)

Cross the road and, over the cattle-grid, go down the access track to Bailton's Farm. Continue down and eventually right through the gated, cobbled yard to cross the bridges over both the motorway and the railway line. (500 metres)

From this last bridge go down the track and, where the hedge on your right ends by a gate, squeeze through the gap stile. If this is blocked go through the gate and subsequent gate. Cross the next field aiming for the distant church tower to reach the right of a lone oak tree standing proud of the far boundary where you can cross a further stile. Directly cross the next short field, aiming left of the pylon, to pass through a gateway over a dyke, and then follow the left-hand boundary to the field corner where you cross the stile and plank footbridge facing you. (400 metres)

[If you want to return to Garstang by the canal towpath you can access it by going through the gate adjacent to this stile and walking a short distance to a canal bridge and steps. (1.5 km)]

Cross the next field, parallel to the canal, aiming to pass through the gate to the right of the farm buildings ahead. Go through the small yard to find a stile to the immediate right of the next gate, over which follow the left-hand hedge along to reach a further stile in the far left-hand corner. A short enclosed path leads to the last stile by the former Greenhalgh Castle Farm. (400 metres)

🛈 The Farm is a seventeenth-century building with stone mullion windows. The stone was 'quarried' from the castle that was built to guard the ford over the Wyre in 1490 by the first earl of Derby. This was one of the last strongholds in Lancashire to hold out against Parliament in the Civil War but access to the site is now restricted.

🚶 Go left along the farm access road to reach the road bridge over the Wyre. Turn right along the road and then, after some 100 metres, go right along the obvious riverside path, signposted Wyre Way, back to the start of the walk. (1 km)

RIVER WYRE – the name of the river gives the name to the local district council. The name is possibly a Celtic derivative of the Welsh 'Gwyar' meaning blood water, a possible description of the reddish-brown peat load carried by the river in spate. The river rises in the Bowland fells above Abbeystead before flowing to the sea at Fleetwood and Knott End.

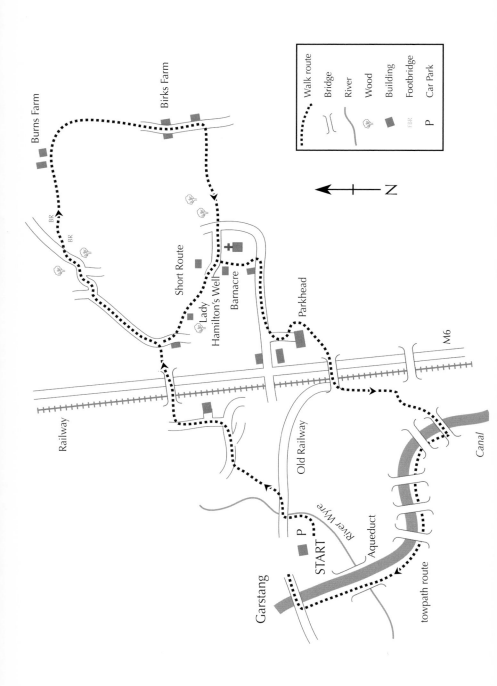

Burns Farm

Birks Farm

N

Walk route

Bridge

River

Wood

Building

FBR Footbridge

P Car Park

BR

BR

Short Route

Lady
Hamilton's Well

Barnacre

Parkhead

M6

Railway

Old Railway

Canal

Garstang

START

P

River Wyre

Aqueduct

towpath route

WALK 11

Exploring Barnacre

Garstang – Barnacre – Lady Hamilton's Well – Garstang

LENGTH:	10.4 km (6.2 miles) Shorter route via Well 7.3 km (4.5 miles)
START:	Garstang Discovery Centre (GR 493454)
BUS:	Garstang lies on the main Preston to Lancaster route (services 40, 41) and Lancaster to Blackpool Route (services 42 and X42)
PARKING:	By Garstang Discovery Centre
MAP:	O.S. Explorer OL41 – Forest of Bowland & Ribblesdale

ⓘ A walk along field paths, quiet lanes and a return along the canal. The full walk and the shorter option both have elevated viewpoints worthy of the minor efforts of the walk.

🚶 **From the Discovery Centre go from the rear of the car park to the river and follow along the sports field-edge path and riverbank towards the bridge, and climb the steps up the near side of the bridge abutment. (400 metres)**

ⓘ The bridge crosses the extraction point from the Lune-Wyre Conjunctive Use Scheme; from here water supplies are piped to the Frank Law Treatment works at Catterall before

Burns Quarry Wood, Barnacre

joining the North West supply grid. The upstream barriers are to prevent flood-waters from inundating villages down stream.

⊛ **Go over the bridge and just after the embankment track has joined from the left go left down steps to cross a stile and then across the field to a further stile. In the next field continue in the same direction to cross a further stile near the right-hand field corner. Go across the next field to meet the left-hand boundary, which is followed to a stile by a gate, and access to Wyre Lane. (500 metres)**

Go right along the lane, fork left at the junction and continue up to meet the metalled road where you turn left. Follow this, pass the farm track on your right and, some 50 metres on at the end of the next field go over the stiled-footbridge to enter the field and follow the left-hand hedge along. Cross the railway footbridge and the following bridge over the motorway. Continue directly up the field to cross two consecutive stiles by gates in the top left-hand field corner. Here you have the choice of two routes. (1.6 km)

The main, longer route goes left along the road, ignores the road (Higher Lane) off to the left and continues up Eidsforth Lane to a further road junction. Turn left here, continue uphill on the road, pass the gated drive on your right and, when almost opposite the far end of the wood on your left, cross a stile on your right. Leave this first field by the footbridge just to your left and then bear half-right, aiming to the right of Burns Farm, to cross the next stiled footbridge. Follow the right-hand boundary up to the farm, cross the two consecutive stiles facing you and then go forward and left to enter the farmyard. (1.5 km)

Turn right in the farmyard and then go right on the gated track which bends almost immediately to the left

and then continues uphill along the track, passes through
a total of three gates before it bends sharp left. Facing
you at this bend is a gate and stile with footpath post in
the right-hand field corner. Cross the stile, signed Birks
Farm, and follow the right-hand fence along, under the
over-head power line, to cross another stile in the far
right-hand field corner.

❶ This is the highest point of the walk and gives an extensive
panorama to the coast.

Ⓧ Cross the next field by aiming for the buildings of Birks
Farm and, at the far side of the field, go down to a
gate and bridge over a stream. Through the gate climb
towards the farm on the track, go through the gated
farmyard (up to four gates across your way) and leave
by following along the farm access road. Continue to
reach the next building (soon to be a house) on your left.
(1.0 km)
   Continue along the access road but, after a further
100 metres or so, look for a stile on your right where
the hedge has a fenced gap. Cross this double stile and
go directly ahead to cross a further stile in the field
boundary across your way. In the following field go down
by the remains of a right-hand ditch and former hedge
line towards the corner of the wood ahead. Follow the
wood, on your right, down over a stile by a gate and
continue to reach the road by a gate and a double stile in
the bottom right-hand field corner. Take the road directly
ahead, Delph Lane, to reach Barnacre Church and the
shorter route described below. (1.1 km)

❶ Barnacre Church has interesting stained glass windows of
saints and, if open, is worth looking inside. Along with
Scorton Church (Walk 4) it is to the design of Paley and
Austin.

(🚶) From the road outside the lower church gate go left up a few steep stone steps to follow the enclosed path, initially between the churchyard and Rushton House. After two stiles walk ahead for 10 metres and cross the stile by the second of two consecutive gates, turn right follow the ditch and hedge along to leave the field by a stile by a gate near the right-hand field corner. (300 metres)

Go right down the metalled Parkhead Lane, pass Clarkson's farm and take the first track to the left by Bayleys. Follow the track along for a short distance but, at the gateway, turn left to cross the stile by the gate, go right along the enclosed track and then climb a stile by a gate in the field above the M6. Over the stile follow the right-hand boundary down to cross the motorway and subsequent railway bridge. A second, stone arched former railway bridge over the disused Pilling Pig line is then crossed by two stiles. (800 metres)

(ℹ️) A short return route to Garstang can be taken from the stile to the near right hand side of this bridge, going steeply left down to the old track-bed, through the permissive path in the 'Wildgoose Reserve' and then straight along to Garstang.

(🚶) Over this second bridge enter the field by a stile and immediately turn left over the next stile. In the field gradually bear away from the left-hand railway-side fence to cross the field, aiming for the distant group of pylons, and to cross a stile some 50 m from the left-hand field corner in the boundary across your way. In the next field turn right to follow the right-hand hedge to cross a largely hidden stile in the far right-hand field corner. Continue by the right-hand hedge, under the over-head power lines to a further stile in the right-hand field corner. Continue ahead to cross the gate in the next

Lancaster Canal, near Castle Farm

right-hand field corner then go ahead along the track to the bridge over the canal. (1.0 km)

Go over the bridge and then down the steps on the right and descend to the canal towpath. With the canal to your right-hand go along the towpath to Garstang. The road bridge (number 62) after the aqueduct is where you leave and cross the canal and go through the town back to your starting point. (2.2 km)

The shorter route via Lady Hamilton's Well

On meeting the road go right, pass Crosby Cottage and continue past the farm buildings until you are opposite the brick built Slack Farm. Turn left, through a gate, to go down a short enclosed track to where it crosses a small stream and then cross the stile on the right. Go half-left over this damp field aiming above the clump of sycamore, holly and alder trees to cross a further stile by the facing wood in the far left-hand corner of this small field. (500 metres) In this clump lies the remains of Lady Hamilton's Well.

Hewitson describes this as 'The Spa Well' where the Hamilton family used to bathe when they stayed at Woodacre Hall (no longer standing). Lady Hamilton moved into the area after the death of her husband and perhaps it was her use of this spring-fed well, with its alleged medicinal properties that has led to its current name.

Climb the steep bank with the wood on your right. At the top of the rise there are extensive views of Morecambe Bay and the Lakeland fells. Continue directly ahead aiming to the right of the stone built house, pass the vegetated and rabbit infested depression of 'Delph Quarry' down on your right, and go to cross a stile, in the fence, which is a right-hand continuation of a stone wall seen ahead. Cross the stile in the lower corner of the field, go down the bottom of the garden by the right-hand fence until you reach a footbridge that enables you to cross the stream and climb the steps to the road outside Barnacre Church. (300 metres) From here rejoin the main walk back to Garstang.

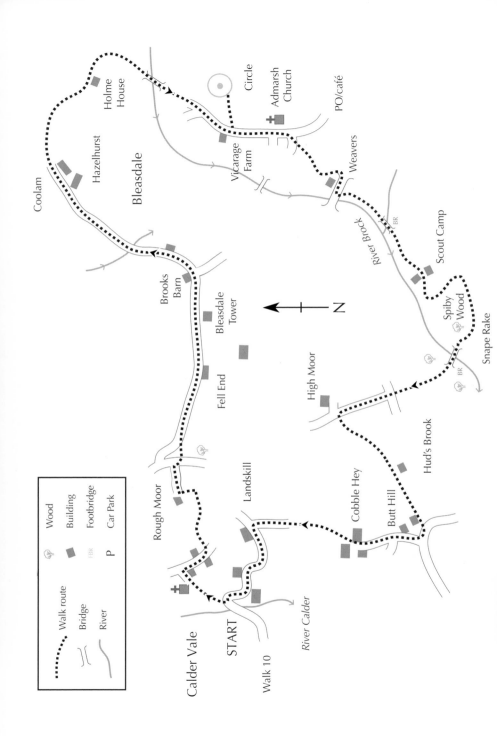

WALK 12

Fellside Parish and Ancient People

Calder Vale – Bleasdale – Calder Vale

LENGTH:	14.5 km (9 miles)
START:	Calder Vale (GR 533458)
BUS:	8C Garstang – Barnacre – Calder Vale (Restricted service and not Sunday)
PARKING:	Politely in the village
MAP:	O.S. Explorer OL41 – Forest of Bowland & Ribblesdale

🛈 This walk combines the best of footpaths near the River Brock (see also Walk 13) as well as a section along the River Calder. It meanders below the fells and through woodlands yet provides excellent views of the fells and the Fylde Plain. The site of a prehistoric 'woodhenge' is visited. Walkers who want a longer ramble can start at Garstang and combine this route with Walk 10 to provide a 24 km (15 mile) circuit. Some paths are often wet but there is several dry-shod km on footpaths over private access tracks. Part of the route is waymarked as Calder Vale Circular walk Red 2. A much shorter route is indicated in the text.

🚶 **Cross the bridge over the River Calder below the shop and go left, with the mill and church to your right, to** follow the road along Long Row cottages. When the road swings right, behind the cottages, carry straight on the sign-posted path (to the Church). The tarmacadamed path leads past the mill lodge, alongside the river and then climbs through the wood to the church and school beyond. (800 metres)

Continue ahead on the access road to a junction and go right (even though sign-posted back to Calder Vale), pass Lower Landskill farm and yard and through the gate beyond the last building. Turn left, through a kissing gate by a gate, and go up the middle of the field, keeping a fenced old quarry to your left, to reach and cross a stone

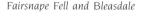

Fairsnape Fell and Bleasdale

St Eadnor, Bleasdale

stile in the top right-hand corner of the field to be found where the wall meets the fence. (500 metres)

Follow the left-hand fence and streamlet up, turn left when the fence bends left to pass through a kissing gate and then aim for a stile to the right of Rough Moor houses. Walk right, up the access track, to a gate through which turn right along the road. After the bend in the road go through a gap stile in the wall on your left (sign-posted) and, after a short section of path through spruce trees, emerge through a small gate into the field. Go up to the access track ahead. (500 metres)

ⓘ During your climb from Calder Vale the views were back across the Fylde Plain to the coast. Now it is towards the fells that off-shoot from the Pennine Chain – the hills of the Forest of Bowland, Longridge Fell, Beacon Fell and, to the south, the heights around Winter Hill.

🚶 **Turn right along the metalled estate road, pass through the gate by Fell End Farm and, after a further gate the rear of Bleasdale Tower that was built as a shooting lodge in the mid-nineteenth century. Continue down the road to a further gate and a junction, and post box, at Brook's Barn Farm. (1.55 km)**

For a shorter return route, missing much of the exciting landscape and history, follow the text of walk 13 from Bleasdale Tower to the road beyond High Moor Farm where the walks re-meet. The shaves some 6 km (3.5 miles) off the route.

Go left by the house and follow the track along passing stone buildings on the right, over a bridge and up through a wood, across a field and arrive at the side of Hazelhurst Farm. (1.25 km).

ⓘ The first houses on the right passed on this stretch were once a reformatory school and the boys, from urban backgrounds, were extensively used as 'inexpensive' estate workers. The bridge you cross (with a date plaque on one face and a mason's stone on the right parapet) was part of their work. They used to turn the fields by hand. Hazelhurst and the adjacent Coolam (whose character has changed in a recent restoration) were once part of a wool producing hamlet inhabited by around 70 people. Most of these were involved in wool spinning and handloom weaving prior to the goods being sent by packhorse to the wool towns of East Lancashire and Yorkshire. The remains of stocks can be noted on your left when approaching the farm.

(𝕏) **From Coolam continue along the track just below the fellside and pass over a gated cattle-grid and continue down the track to reach the rear of Holme House Farm. Go through the gate, directly through the yard and then through a further gate before following a farm track along and over a bridge. This track continues by a right-hand wall where it becomes a 'concessionary' path, it crosses a stream and then follows a left-hand fence to a gate and stile near to Admarsh Barn Farm. Over the stile go directly ahead to pick up the farm access road. Go along this road to cross a cattle grid and, on the right, the access to Vicarage Farm. (1.75 km)**

Over the cattle-grid look for the sign to Bleasdale Circle to your left. To reach the circle site go through the kissing-gate, cross this field by the left-hand fence and go up to a further kissing gate in the top left-hand field corner, and then cross to a further kissing-gate in the clump of trees that hide the circle site. Return by this route to the estate road. (750 metres)

❶ The circle site is marked now by unsightly concrete stumps where once eleven wooden posts stood. In the central area was a small barrow whose excavation yielded graves with two cremations in collared urns and an incense cup. A ditch and a timber palisade surrounded the 50 metre circle. This unique woodhenge site has been dated at various times but the on-site information suggests around 1700 BC. The entrance to the circle points towards the Fairsnape ridge where lies the man-made gouge into the ridge called 'Nicks Chair'. Was it a contemporary alignment with the circle?

(𝕏) **From Vicarage Farm continue along the access road to reach Admarsh Church and then continue down to the village hall (on the left) and school (right) just beyond which is a road junction. (750 metres)**

Brook Farm

ℹ This is a nineteenth-century church building with a 'quaint' Last Supper over the altar and two odd faces peering from carvings on old chairs. It is the only known dedication to St. Eadnor who possibly was the Eadbert who carried on St. Cuthbert's work at Lindisfarne and was buried in the saint's tomb.

🚶 Just after the school turn right and follow this metalled access road until you reach the first gate with stone gate posts on your left. Go through the gate to enter the field and aim for the lower farm buildings. On your way you meet a fence corner and where you continue in the same direction with the fence on your right. This leads to a gate and then, via a short enclosed track, through the gated yard of Weaver's farm and on to the road. (750 metres)

Cross the road diagonally right, and climb the bank to follow the path into a steep-sided wood. Follow along the left-hand boundary fence and after 200 metres cross a stile over to your left to go into the field. Turn right and go down the field by the right-hand fence adjacent to the wood, over a further stile, and then cross a stile on your right by the far corner of the wood. The path now descends steeply near the right-hand fence, crosses a small field to reach a footbridge, Jack Anderton's Bridge, over the eastern branch of the River Brock. (550 metres)

Walk downstream near the right-hand fence, pass through a gate and then at the end of the next field continue over one of two adjacent stiles to enter the grounds of Wood Top Scout Camp. Follow along the wide path until the some 20 metres before the path reaches the near-side of the camp toilet block and begins to climb. (550 metres)

Veer right into the open grassy area and continue with the River Brock down to your right. This path becomes distinct as it re-enters the wood and you shortly arrive at a footpath way-mark post. Turn left here, over a short, flat and wet section of path. The path then steeply climbs left through the wood to reach a seat. The path here bends to the right where you climb more gently to a gate and a road, Snape Rake Lane.

🛈 The wood here is called Spiby Wood, formerly and aptly named Boggy Wood. This was a favourite spot of the late Cyril Spiby, a Preston Rambler and guidebook writer

🚶 Turn right to go along the lane, at first metalled, and then descend the rougher lane to the footbridge and ford over the River Brock. This lane may have been the route of the Roman Road from Ribchester to Lancaster. (1.25 km)

☞ Cross the footbridge and climb Snape Rake up to cross a stile by a gate, and then follow the more level track through an avenue of trees to reach a gate and road junction. (500 metres)

Follow the Oakenclough road (Delph Lane) straight ahead and after about 600 metres cross a stone step stile in the left hand wall diagonally opposite the entrance drive to High Moor Farm. [This is where you re-meet the short-cut from Bleasdale Tower.] Cross the field diagonally left to aim for an obvious woodland to cross the fence by a stile by a gate. In the next field aim just to the right of the centre of the enclosed wood. Enter the wood by a stone step stile, follow the path directly across the Huds Brook Wood and then re-enter the fields by a further stone step stile. (1.25 km)

Cross the next field aiming some 30 metres to the right of the farm buildings to cross a piped section of ditch and then reaching a stile with a tall marker post in the hedge across your way. Cross the track and subsequent stile and then continue in the same direction in the next field, passing the left-hand farm buildings and keeping parallel to the left-hand wall to find a kissing-gate to the right of a short line of trees. Go to cross a further stile seen shortly ahead. Climb the slight rise in the next field and then descend to cross an obvious stile, track and stile below you. Go down the next field alongside the right-hand boundary to reach a road by a stile adjacent to the gate in the far right-hand field corner. (650 metres)

Turn right along the road but shortly turn right again along the access track to Butt Hill and Cobble Hey farms. Keep along the concrete track to pass Infield house and Sullom View to your left and continue over the cattle-grid by the tarmac access road to reach the cobbled yard of Cobble Hey farm and gardens. (1.0 km) The tea rooms are open most days (telephone 01995 602643 to check in advance).

Suitably refreshed continue through the yard, pass the farmhouse and go through the gate on your right. Follow a track by the right-hand wall of the gardens to where the gardens end and the track bends right into a field. Your way is to pass through the gate directly ahead. Go through this field by initially keeping near the right-hand wall but, as this begins to bend away to the right, go more directly ahead and down the field towards a lightly treed hollow, to a find a gate in the hollow where a wall and fence meet. Note the oak way-mark stone. Go through this gate, over the stream, and keep on the sunken track near the right-hand fence and eventually up to pass through a further gate and its curlew way-mark stone. In the next field follow the right-hand fence as it bends round (a flower way-mark stone) and leads you to pass through a further gate (bull way-mark) beyond which an enclosed track leads to the Landskill farms. (800 metres)

Turn left after the gate by the first farmhouse on your left and then go down through the gate, past the elegant front of the vernacular Jacobean farmhouse where once Catholics held forbidden services. The farm access road continues down a lane which turns right through a field and then left by some buildings. It leads down to Long Row and to the centre of Calder Vale. (750 metres)

THE FOREST OF BOWLAND received its name not from woodland cover but because it was covered by laws applying to its status as a Royal Forest. These game preserves were set up largely after the Norman Conquest. The Forest Law could be harsh on local residents especially if they had been poaching. This part of Lancashire had a number of hunting forests. The upper reaches of the Wyre were, for example, part of the Royal Forest of Wyresdale.

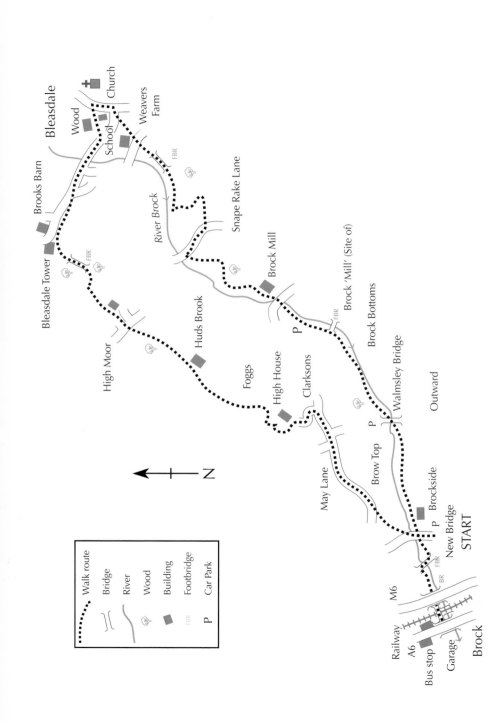

WALK 13

The Badger's River

Brock – Bleasdale – Claughton – Brock

LENGTH:	17.4 km (11 miles) or for bus users 20 km (12.5 miles) – but see text below for shorter alternatives
START:	New Bridge (GR: 523410) or the other car parks. Public transport users start at Brock (A6 -GR 512406). The walk can also be started from other car parks (see box)
BUS:	Service 40 & 41 LANCASTER – GARSTANG – PRESTON SERVICE TO BROCK – stop near garage.
PARKING:	By the A6 is difficult. Cars can be easily parked at the Brock Mill (also called Brock Bottoms) Picnic Site (SD 549430) or a few can find roadside space at either New Bridge (SD 523410) or Walmsley Bridge (SD 533415).
MAP:	O.S. Explorer Sheet OL41 Forest of Bowland and Ribblesdale

ⓘ The middle and upper reaches of the River Brock are a long time favourite area for Lancashire ramblers'. Much of the river can be followed close to its banks, there is delightful scenery and good opportunities of seeing river birds such as dipper, wagtails or kingfisher but, as it banks are well wooded, the river often has a secretive appearance. The higher fields are the haunt of curlews and sandpipers whilst pheasants are abundant at the upper reaches. Many of the paths can be very muddy, and some of the fields on the return route can be damp. The walk is an excellent stroll up the river especially in autumn when the riverside woodlands are at their best.

From New Bridge pass through a gap stile (footpath sign to Walmsley bridge) adjacent to the track to Brock Side and follow the enclosed path by the riverbank until it comes to a stile at the end of the buildings. Once rural fields and a farm, Brock Side is now a suburbanised housing development. From the stile cross the mown area and go to cross the next stile by the gate. In the field follow the long left-hand fence above the river and leave it by the stile and gate at the far end (note the small waterfall in the Brock). Continue on a track by the left-hand hedge, cross another two stiles by gates, and in the next field keep on the track by a line of trees to reach Walmsley Bridge by a further stile by a gate. (1.4km)

Go left to cross Walmsley Bridge and immediately re-enter a field by the kissing gate (footpath sign to Brock Bottoms) on your right. This next part of the route is waymarked as Calder Vale Blue Walk 2 as far as Snape Rake Lane. Cross the field to avoid the meander of the river and then pass through a short wood with kissing gates at each end. Cross the next field keeping parallel to the left-hand fence but as the field narrows go over the stile near the river. Follow the riverbank path along, cross the stile and gate of a temporary enclosure, again at a narrowing of the field, and continue near the bank until an old hedge-bank comes down towards you. Go to the left of this hedge and follow the right-hand side of the hedge up to pass through a kissing gate by a gate to reach a track. (1.0km)

Go right down the track, pass the of the site of former

Brock Corn Mill – later making files for metalworkers – continue along a path with the river near to your right for some distance. You pass through open spaces and woodlands and eventually emerge on the road at Brock Mill by Higher Brock Bridge adjacent to the Brock Bottoms picnic site, nature trail and car park. (1.3km)

Go over the bridge and immediately turn left to pass through the gap stile by the gateway. Keep left below Brock Mill house and the adjacent Brock Mill Cottage and then climb the stile by the gate. Go by the right-hand boundary and then almost immediately turn right as it bends right. When the boundary bends again continue directly ahead to pick up the left-hand fence adjacent to the river. Follow this fence along and cross the stile in the far left-hand corner of the field. The path now continues between the river and the right-hand fence until, at the far end of the field to your right, the path bends away from the river, climbs through a narrow wood and up the short bluff beyond to reach a track. Go left down the track and just above the former cottage, with the aqueduct to your left, leave the track to the right to enter the edge of the wood. The path now follows the fence line at the bottom of the wood, with a field to your left, to eventually emerge on the river bank. Follow this along to meet the footbridge over the Brock and where Snape Rake Lane crosses the river. (1.3km)

A shorter route can be taken by crossing the river, as described in walk 12, and rejoining our route near Huds Brook Farm.

Go right and up the sunken hollow of Snape Rake Lane. Continue along it when it becomes tarred, cross its highest point, and as the wood on your left gives way to a field, turn left through two stone gate posts and then a wooden gate. Follow the track down through the wood, continue as it bends back sharp left and then bears right to meet a track along the flatter ground nearer the river.

Bleasdale from the slopes of Parlick Pike

Go right along the track, leave the wood to pass through
a small field and go towards the toilet block of the Scout
Camp Activity Centre. Go left on the track here and
continue through the remainder of the camp-site and
wood to cross a stile just after the track ends. (1.3km)

Cross the field parallel to the right-hand wood and
continue, through the gate, in the next field towards
a footbridge at the confluence of the two infant Brock
rivers. Cross the footbridge and continue by the left-hand

fence to the end of the open field. The path now climbs
steeply by the fence to a stile, ignore the other stile to
your left, facing you. Cross this stile, enter the field and
go left, by the fence at the edge of the wood, to cross
a further stile in the far left-hand corner of the field.
Continue by the left-hand fence for around 50 metres
until a stile appears in the fence. Cross this and turn
right to follow the top of the wood along before the
path eventually descends to the road opposite Weavers'
Farm. (1.0km)

Bleasdale

Cross the road directly to the yard of the farm, enter the yard to the right of the farmhouse and follow the gated track that bears slightly right through the farmyard and back out into a field. Follow the left-hand fence through the field until it bends left but you continue directly ahead towards an obvious gate and subsequent lane. Go right on the lane and then left at the junction to continue past the school, village hall to reach the church. (900 metres) See Walk 12 if you wish to add Bleasdale Circle to you visit. The church is worthy of a short visit.

Continue just beyond the church, cross the cattle-grid and then turn immediately left to pass over a second cattle-grid, pass the house, once the 1720 former Admarsh Barn, and leave by the facing gate. Follow the track down the field, pass by the left-hand side of a small Scots pine copse, and continue down to cross a stile by a gate. Beyond the gate a short track leads to the estate road which you follow to the right, cross the Brock by Brooks Farm, with its saddle (packhorse) bridge to your right, and continue upwards (ignoring any left turns) until you reach a right-hand road turning off at Brooks Barn Farm. (1.6km)

This next section of the walk is waymarked as Calder Vale Blue Walk 2 and Red Walk 2 as far as Butt Hill. Leave the road by the second of two gates on your left (opposite Brooks Barn house), go along a short track, through a gate, along by the left-hand fence below Bleasdale Tower, and through a further gate to enter a large field. Turn half left and go down and across this wet field to an obvious gate half-way down the facing wood. Through the gate follow the track through the narrow wood and, via gates, to reach the yard of Broadgate Farm. Turn left by the first building and follow a track that bends right and joins the main farm access track. Go straight across this access track to cross a stile by a gate. Go up the field near the left-hand fence to

pass through a kissing gate in the top left-hand corner of
the field by the buildings at High Moor Farm. Continue
through the facing kissing gate and then follow the
boundary of the garden to the rear of the house along
and left to a field gate. Go left on the access track to the
metalled road. (2.0km) Those taking the short cut from
Snape Rake Lane rejoin our walk here.

Go diagonally left across the road to climb a stone
stile and enter a field. Cross the field diagonally left to
aim for an obvious woodland to cross the fence by a stile
by a gate. In the next field aim just to the right of the
centre of the enclosed wood. Enter the wood by a stone
step stile, follow the path directly across the Huds Brook
Wood and then re-enter the fields by a further stone
step stile. Cross the next field aiming some 30 metres to
the right of the farm buildings to cross a piped section
of ditch and then reaching a stile with a tall marker
post in the hedge across your way. Cross the track and
subsequent stile and then continue in the same direction
in the next field, passing the left-hand farm buildings and
keeping parallel to the left-hand wall to find a kissing-
gate to the right of a short line of trees. Go to cross a
further stile seen shortly ahead. Climb the slight rise in
the next field and then descend to cross and obvious
stile, track and stile below you. Go down the next field
alongside the right-hand boundary to reach a road by
a stile adjacent to the gate in the far right-hand field
corner. (1.6km)

The next section of the walk is also waymarked as
Calder Vale Blue Walk 2. Cross the road directly and
enter the field by the stile by the gate. Go half-left to
climb the hillock passing a bent oak tree, and then
descend following the overhead power lines to reach
a gate in the farm track, a short distance to the left of
Foggs Farm buildings. Go through the gate and cross
the track directly to a kissing gate and enter the field

Snape Rake Lane, Brock

to again follow the overhead lines. Cross the stile in the facing boundary which is found to the right of the last power line pole. Again follow the route of the power lines to find a slightly hidden stile, adjacent to another pole, which you cross to gain the corner of a further field. Go right in the field and follow near the right-hand fence along to a gate and the road. (1.0km)

Turn right along the road but very soon leave it to the left to go along the gated access track of High House Farm. Follow the track and just after it bends left go through the gate on your right into a field. Turn half-left across the field aiming for a gate in the boundary to the right of a prominent oak at the highest part of the field. Go through this gate and turn left to go to cross a further stile, situated between two gates, and over which you follow the right-hand fence to a further stile.

Cross the stile and follow the left-hand boundary down to a gate in the far left-hand corner at the bottom of the field. This enables you to follow an enclosed track until your way is crossed by a gate. Here go over the stile to your left to enter the grounds of a house where you go to reach the road by the access drive to Clarkson's Farm. Turn right along the road, May Lane, and follow this for some 1300 metres, ignoring roads off to the left and then right, until you come to a right-hand bend by Brow Top. (2.5km)

ℹ️ If you want a short cut back to the Brock Mill or Walmsley Bridge starting points you can continue to follow the Calder Vale Blue Walk 2 down a road to Walmsley Bridge Road.

🚶 **Just past the access track to the house, the stone built Brow Top, continue on the road for some 20 metres to find a gap in the stone wall on your left. Go through this, pass over the garden and between the two houses and, beyond the far-end of the right-hand house go over a stile to enter a field. Go half-right to contour around the hilly field, and then follow near to the right-hand boundary before crossing to the left towards the white house and a stile to the road. Turn left on the road and immediately over New Bridge. Those returning by bus will have to retrace your original steps along the Brock to the A6 at Brock. (500 metres).**

A VACCARY is a small settlement were cattle were bred and land farmed on the King's behalf in the twelfth and thirteenth centuries. Names of these settlements are still in use today. In upper Wyresdale there were twelve vaccaries and examples met on the walks include Tarnbrook, Catshaw, Emmott, Marshaw and Haythornthwaite. Others existed in Bleasdale.

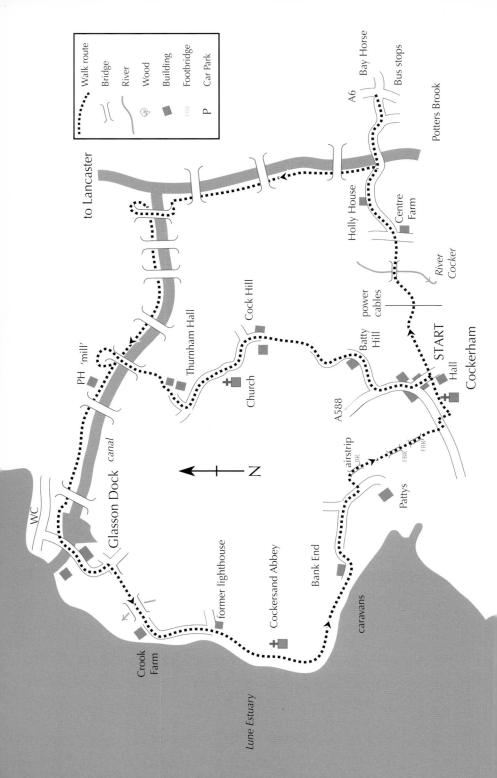

Legend

- ▪▪▪ Walk route
-)(Bridge
- River
- 🌳 Wood
- ▪ Building
- FBR Footbridge
- P Car Park

to Lancaster

Glasson Dock *canal*

WC

Crook Farm

Lune Estuary

former lighthouse

Cockersand Abbey

Bank End

caravans

Pattys

FBR

FBR

airstrip

A588

Hall

Cockerham

START

Batty Hill

Church

Cock Hill

Thurnham Hall

PH 'mill'

power cables

River Cocker

Centre Farm

Holly House

A6

Bay Horse

Bus stops

Potters Brook

N

WALK 14

Of Water and Abbots

Cockerham – Bay Horse – Glasson Dock – Cockerham

LENGTH:	16.5 km (10 miles) or 13 km (8 miles) shorter route
START:	Cockerham centre (GR 465523). Alternatively Glasson Dock can be used. Bus passengers from Garstang and the south can alight at Bay Horse/ Potters Brook but only for the longer route.
BUS:	Cockerham is served by the 89 Lancaster to Knott End buses. Bay Horse/Potters Brook is on the Lancaster–Garstang–Preston Service 40 & 41 route and the 42 Lancaster to Blackpool via Garstang service.
PARKING:	In Cockerham near Parish Hall
MAP:	O.S. Explorer 296 – Lancaster, Morecambe & Fleetwood

ℹ This walk has a variety of interests especially the most scenic sections of the Lancaster Canal and the Lancashire Coast at the Lune estuary. Glasson Dock and Cockersand Abbey feature on both routes whilst the shorter route offers Thurnham Hall at the expense of some excellent canal walking. This walk includes a section of the Lancashire Coastal Way.

Canal Junction, Galgate

From Manor Inn in the centre of Cockerham walk south along the road and turn onto the footpath immediately adjacent to house number 27. Go through the short garden, climb the stile and then through the gate by the top right of the barn. In the field follow the right-hand hedge up the hillock, a drumlin. (200 metres)

From this rise there are extensive views of Wyresdale, Morecambe Bay, the Lakeland Fells and south towards Winter Hill.

⊛ Descend the hillock to cross a stile where the right-hand hedge kinks at the base of the hillock. Now follow the hedge on your left and cross a stile facing you just right of the field corner. Cross the next field diagonally to the gate in the far right-hand corner, by the corner of a small wood, go over the stile and footbridge by the gate, turn left and climb the stile by the next gate. In the next field aim for the left-hand corner of the wood ahead, pass under the overhead power line and cross a footbridge over the River Cocker. (700 metres)

Follow up the right-hand edge of the wood, pass through a gateway and go over the stile that almost immediately follows on your right. Go up the field along the left-hand hedge and through the gate facing you in the top left-hand corner. Diagonally cross the middle of the next field to pass through a gate at the rear of Centre Farm. (450 metres)

Go to follow the track ahead, with the farm buildings on your right. The enclosed track becomes metalled at Holly House Farm and then leads down to the canal. (1.1 km) Those using the bus along the A6 at Bay Horse/ Potters Brook will join and leave the walk here – the bus stop is a short distance over the canal bridge.

The canal is now followed northwards, the water on your right, until it comes to the high-arched bridge over the Glasson branch. Cross the bridge and turn down left to follow the seven-locked branch to reach Glasson Dock. (6.4 km)

❶ The canal stretch has adjacent woods, a rock cutting through the local sandstone, an attractive canal junction and has boating activity and wildlife along the way. The Lancaster canal runs between the 50 and 100 foot contours and was built following a 1792 Act of Parliament. Its main users were industrial, agricultural and passenger traffic. Boats carried cargoes of coal north from Wigan and limestone south from Kendal. The bridges are a typical elliptical design of the builder, Rennie.

🛈 On our way to Glasson Dock we pass Thurnham Mill, now a hotel and bar. It was a water-powered corn mill driven by turbines and with a drying kiln on its north side. Water was taken from the canal, the race can be seen, but was originally extracted from the River Conder.

🛈 Glasson Dock is largely a product of the canal age and developed when increasing size of ships and silting of the Lune prevented ships using St George's Quay in Lancaster. The main dock was constructed by 1791 and was large enough to hold 25 large merchant ships. Some of the trade was with the West Indies. The branch canal was opened to the dock in 1826 and is notable for its wooden lock footbridges and the side weirs at the locks. The railway link with Lancaster took away the canal trade but today the port is still commercially used, including trade with the Isle of Man, and the village relies to some degree on tourism – especially at weekends.

⊛ **The next section of the walk follows the well way-marked Lancashire Coastal Way. From the lock swing-bridge, by the port, follow the road up Tithebarn Hill to the viewpoint with an indicator and fine views across the estuary to Sunderland. Turn left on the road at the top and then go right, into Marsh Lane, at the next cross roads near the farm with two prominent silo towers. Go down the enclosed lane and pass through a gate just beyond the caravan site entrance. (550 metres)**
    After passing through a second gate follow the track across the field, initially by the right-hand hedge line, then bear left to pass over a gated bridge before you continue along the track by a further right-hand hedge to reach the rear of Crook Farm. Go through the gate and

pass to the left of the farm buildings and then follow the
farm access road to the left, along the Lune estuary, to a
road junction by Lighthouse Cottage. (1.75 km) The area
of the Lune and Cocker estuaries is a bird sanctuary and
in winter can provide a spectacle of many thousands of
waders.

Continue along the estuary-side track, go through a
kissing gate by a gate, along the edge of the sea defence
wall, and via a series of two more kissing gates to reach
the ruin of Cockersand Abbey, and then eventually, just
before the war-time look-out building, descend by a
concrete ramp to a small gate and the shoreline path at
Bank House. (1.75 km)

🛈 The remains of Cockersand Abbey with its remaining
Chapter House was a site established by the
Premonstratensian Order in 1190 where there had
previously been the abode of hermit Hugh Garth in 1180
– possible an island site amongst salt marshes – before
it became a hospital colony for lepers and the infirm.
Dissolution came in 1539 when the house contained 22
priests, five aged and infirm men who were *kept dayle
of charitie*, and 57 servants. The Chapter House (c1230),
with its vaulted roof held by clustered columns and leafy
capitals, later became a burial vault for the Dalton family of
Thurnham. The Dalton's were probably responsible for the
crenellation.

🚶 **Continue to keep on the edge of the foreshore to the
road end at Cockerham Sands Caravan Park and continue
on the seaward edge, via a small gate to reach a tarred
road at Bank End Farm. Go ahead to follow the access
road besides the embankment, turn right at the junction
at the far end, and continue on a road towards Pattys
Farm and the parachute centre. Just before the final
right-hand bend before the farm turn left up the first of**

two pairs of steps up the embankment. (2.25 km) Here we leave the Lancashire Coastal Way.

Climb the stile from the embankment and go by the right-hand fence to shortly cross a further stile and footbridge. In the field, with the buildings of the parachute centre to the right, aim towards Cockerham Church to reach and cross a stile by a gate. In the next three fields, connected by footbridges, follow the left-hand fence and dyke and, at the end of the third field, go over a stile in the far left-hand field corner that gives access to the road. (800 metres)

Thurnham Hall

Cockersand Abbey Chapter House

Go left along the road and, just before the road climbs
to Cockerham village, pass through the white kissing gate
and follow a made path that leads to the corner of the
churchyard. The church was rebuilt in 1910 by Paley and
Austin and has some plague gravestones. Go through the
next white kissing gate, follow the right-hand wall of the
churchyard and then go left up the church access track
to the Parish Hall and the centre of the village, the start
of the walk lies to the left. (400 metres)

Shorter Route

The shorter route often has some wet patches of path
but it enables a view of Thurnham Church and Thurnham
Hall. From the Manor Inn go north on the Lancaster road

(A588) and continue along the road after the pavement ends. It may be safer to walk on the opposite side of the road. Just after Batty Cottage turn right to follow the track to Batty Hill Farm. Go through the yard and, immediately after the front of the farmhouse, take the left branch of the track and go down the enclosed lane to pass through a gate. (800 metres)

The track follows the right-hand field boundary and, in the far right-hand corner, goes through the left of two gates to continue to a further gate tucked away in the far right-hand corner. Go through this gate and two further gates on this short enclosed track to enter a field. Turn into the field and cross the middle of the field by aiming towards the pylon directly inline and behind the extensive buildings of Cock Hall Farm. Cross the boundary on your way by a footbridge stile and go to the yard of the farm just to the right of the first building. Pass between the buildings, with the house on your right, and continue to join the farm access road. (700 metres)

From Cock Hall Farm follow the access road and eventually pass the Roman Catholic Church and then continue to find Thurnham Hall on your right. (1.15 km) The remote Roman Catholic Thurnham Church with its Egyptian style tomb is worth a few minutes look if the door is open.

ⓘ Thurnham Hall was once the home of the Dalton family who were descended from Sir Thomas More and the house was originally a thirteenth century pele tower and the centre of a 50,000 acre estate. In the sixteenth century it was altered to look like a small castle and it acquired a new front (the original wall is behind) and a chapel in the nineteenth century. In the wall is a three-hundred year old vow, likely brought from Aldcliffe Hall 'We are the Catholic virgins who scorn to change with the times' – the vow of two of eleven Dalton sisters during Protestant rule.

The façade of the house is attractive but the extensive commercial activities of this time-share/country club detract from the rural setting. The conversion of an interesting eighteenth-century barn for holiday homes is much to be regretted.

(🚶) **Turn right and go down the road to pass parallel to the face of the house but, when this track bends left continue ahead over the grass, past the former barn and beyond which you turn right through the length of the car park. Cross over a stile hidden behind the ash tree and, in the field, go directly ahead to meet and follow the remains of an old hedged lane by a gate and continue down to pass through over the stile by the gate at the end of the this track. Turn right in the next field and go away from the right-hand boundary towards a railed bridge, Baileys Bridge, over the canal. Cross the bridge and, before the next wooden stile that faces you, turn left to squeeze through the gap in the left hand corner and descend the steps to the towpath. Follow the canal, with the water on your left, to pass Thurnham Mill and on to reach Glasson Dock. (2.75 km) On meeting the canal towpath you have joined the longer route.**

PUBLIC TRANSPORT – most of the walks in this book are accessible from public transport. The service numbers are given with each walk. For up to date travel information you are strongly advised to telephone for times prior to travel. The relevant number is 0871 200 22 33 (ask for Lancashire if you phone from outside the county). Information about the running of Fleetwood and Knott End Ferry can be obtained from Fleetwood Tourist Information Centre 01253 773953.

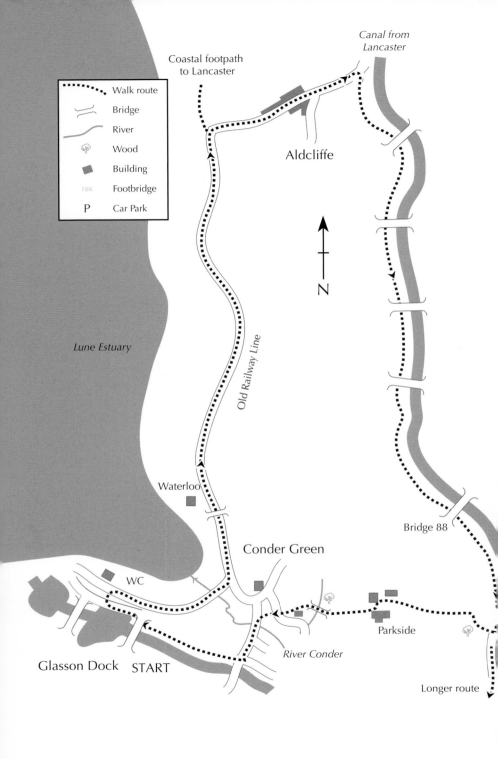

Walk route
Bridge
River
Wood
Building
FBR Footbridge
P Car Park

Canal from Lancaster

Coastal footpath to Lancaster

Aldcliffe

N

Lune Estuary

Old Railway Line

Waterloo

Bridge 88

Conder Green

WC

Parkside

Glasson Dock START

River Conder

Longer route

WALK 15

When Canals and Railways Held Sway

Glasson Dock – Aldcliffe – Galgate – Glasson Dock

LENGTH:	14 km (8.5 miles) – with two extensions suggested in the text
START:	Glasson Dock (GR 445562)
BUS:	89 Lancaster to Knott End. Alternatively start in Lancaster
PARKING:	Readily available in Glasson Dock
MAP:	O.S. Explorer 296 – Lancaster, Morecambe & Fleetwood

ⓘ This walk is mostly along the route of an old railway track-bed and along the canal that are linked by a quiet lane and field-paths. It is a walk for all seasons but spring and autumn give life to the canal side woods, and winter brings the birds to the estuary. The walk features transport through the ages and there is often much wildlife to see especially along the Lune Estuary. The walk is mostly level and very suitable for those who do not wish to concentrate too much on finding their way. Part of this walk is used by the Lancashire Coastal Path.

ⓘ As a further alternative this walk can be started at Lancaster. From Lancaster go to join the canal towpath to the south of the city centre and then continue along the towpath which is used after Aldcliffe (p125). To return to Lancaster follow the route until to the bottom of Railway Crossing Lane at Aldcliffe and follow the sign-posted Lancashire Coastal Path along the embankment and then along to St George's Quay into Lancaster. This adds some 5 km (3 miles) to the walk.

From Glasson Dock go to the estuary side at the rear of the public toilets near the Victoria Hotel and, with the estuary on your left, walk along the route of the old railway and modern flood defences. Continue through Conder Green car park and picnic site, the route is now labelled The River Lune Millennium Park, until you eventually reach the metalled road and information board just below Aldcliffe village at the bottom of Railway Crossing Lane. (5500 metres)

For people with a map a field path cuts the last section of the track and part of the road walking up to Aldcliffe. It starts opposite the footpath sign to Aldcliffe Hall Lane.

The railway line from Lancaster to Glasson Dock was opened in 1890 and carried passenger services until 1930. It closed to freight in 1947 but the tracks were not raised until 1962. The only claim to fame of the line was in 1917 when King George V slept overnight on the royal train at Glasson. Trains to the dock were notorious for shaking a row of cottages near the port.

Tales were told of railway firemen who used to kick our lumps of coal from their cabs when passing a fisherman's hut. Sometimes a salmon made the return journey. One engine driver was demoted after arriving at Lancaster only to discover that his carriages had been left behind at Glasson Dock station.

There were stations at Conder Green and a private one

used by Lord Aston at Ashton Hall where you can still find the overgrown remains of the timber platform. Birdwatchers will need binoculars along this estuary side path.

🚶 **Our way goes right up the metalled road through the village of Aldcliffe. At the top of the village go left at the road junction and follow the road down to meet the canal. Turn right, with the water on your left, to follow the towpath south all the way to the outskirts of Galgate which is marked, some 500 metres after bridge 89, by the edge of an estate of houses and bungalows on the far bank of the canal. (5600 metres) The route from Lancaster is on the towpath that is used from Aldcliffe.**

🛈 This well wooded section of the canal is especially attractive in spring and autumn as the canal passes through a three km cutting to avoid the need for locks. The Lancaster Canal ran from Preston to Tewitfield for forty-eight km before the first and only flight of locks to Kendal was reached. The bridges you pass under are fine half-elliptical arches, examples of the work of the canal builder John Rennie. Another bridge you cross over is where a stream is syphoned under the canal.

🚶 **For a slightly longer route instead of turning off the canal continue along the towpath until you reach the canal junction. Turn right and follow the Glasson branch of the canal all the way down to the start. This adds about 2.5 km (1.5 miles) to the walk.**

Once opposite these dwellings of Galgate turn right to cross a wooden stile in the hedge on your right. Go diagonally right across the field to pass over a stile by a gate in the boundary adjacent to the side of the wood. Continue with the wood on your left and cross the next stile on your left to enter the wood where the wood narrows. (250 metres)

Glasson Dock

Ascend the path through the narrow Forerigg Wood and leave by the stile at the far side. In the field climb straight up the short, steep slope with a pylon seen ahead and then descend to cross the iron stile in a dip by the left of three trees in the boundary facing you. (250 metres)

Follow the right-hand hedge over a further stile, under the overhead power lines and, when close to the farm, cross through a stone gap stile by a gate in the right-hand hedge. In this next field turn left and descend to the yard of Parkside Farm. Pass through the gate adjacent to the

right-hand concrete-walled silage clamp wall, turn left
and then immediately right. From here go straight ahead
to cross a stile by gate, adjacent to an over-head wire
pole, in the boundary facing. (370 metres)

Follow the right-hand boundary in the next field, cross
a stile by a gate and continue to cross a stile in the far
right-hand corner of the second field adjacent to Crow
Wood. Go ahead to cross the stone slab footbridge and
then over a stile on your right. In the next field turn
left and follow the left hand hedge up to pass through
a gate and then down the next field to pass the rear
of Webster's Farm and reach the road by a stile in the
bottom left-hand corner of the field and to the left of the
small electricity sub station building. (750 metres)

Go ahead on the road, turn left and follow the main
road, with care, over the river bridge and then to the
canal bridge. Go down left to the canal towpath and then
turn right to go under the bridge and follow the towpath
to return to your start at Glasson Dock. (2000 metres)

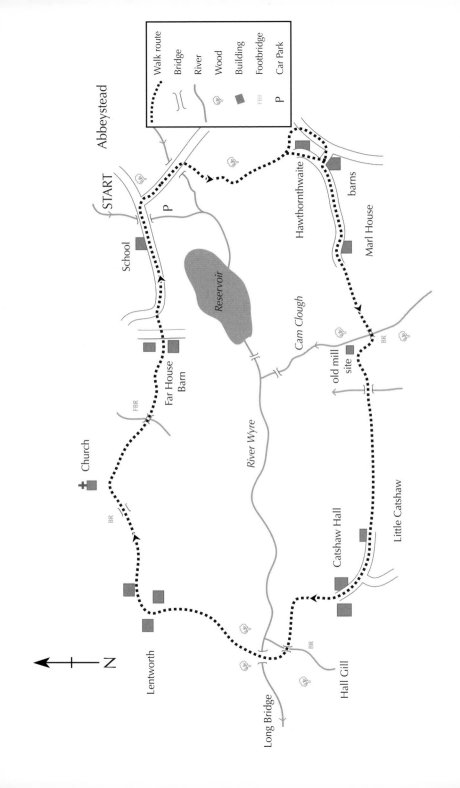

WALK 16

The Shepherd's Church of Wyresdale

Abbeystead – Hawthornthwaite – Catshaw – The Shepherd's Church – Abbeystead

LENGTH:	5.5 km (3.5 miles)
START:	Abbeystead Stoops Bridge (GR 563543)
BUS:	Service 146 or 147 Lancaster to Abbeystead
PARKING:	Stoops Bridge – to the east of the school
MAP:	O.S. Explorer OL41 – Forest of Bowland & Ribblesdale

❶ A superb, short walk around Upper Wyresdale amongst the fields and woods adjacent to Walk 2 of the book but rarely using the same paths. The two walks provide an excellent complement to Walk 1. This walk, suitable for most times of the year, visits Wyresdale Church, better known as the Shepherd's Church and provides delightful views of the River Wyre and the Abbeystead Reservoir. Abbeystead is named after the short-lived Cistercian Abbey that was probably sited at the confluence of the Marshaw and Tarnbrook Wyres by monks from Furness Abbey. After a short period, during the twelfth century, the monks moved on to Ireland. Camden describes the scene here as 'solitary and dismal'. You may find solitude but the landscape is never dismal.

Waymark below Abbeystead Church

From Stoops Bridge, over the Tarnbrook Wyre, continue downstream on the road and cross the next bridge over the Marshaw Wyre. (150 metres) Just below the bridge the two upper Wyre streams combine to carry their waters from the Bowland Fells down to Morecambe Bay.

Immediately over the bridge drop down right to follow the path through the woods. Some 10 metres after the second small footbridges go left on the right of way, ignoring a permissive path that carries straight on, and climb the wooded bluff up a series of steps. On top bear right to cross a stile by a gate and enter a field. (250 metres)

Go left in the field and follow the left-hand fence
along the wood and depression and cross the stile
between two gates. Cross the next field to go through
the gate in the far left-hand corner and then along the
right-hand fence to Hawthornthwaite Farm. The right of
way passes, through a small gate, to the immediate right
of farmhouse but arrows encourage the walker down to
the left and then around the house. Past the house, go
right on the track and soon bend left to go towards the

A *Shepherd window, Abbeystead Church*

modern farm buildings. Go to the right at the nearside of
these buildings and follow the track along to reach Marl
House Farm. (1000 metres)

ⓘ From this track are extensive views of the amphitheatre
of the upper Wyre catchment and Abbeystead House,
the shooting home of the Duke of Westminster, set in its
woodland setting by the river.

ⓧ Continue along the track to the right of the farmhouse,
pass through two consecutive gates facing you and cross
the stile by the gate facing you. In the next field follow
parallel to the left-hand fence and then descend to a stile
and footbridge over the interesting beck in Cam Clough.
(400 metres) The rocks of the bed of Cam Clough show
the wonderful carving action of the down rushing stream.
The smoothness, texture and shape are worth pausing to
see.

Climb the few steps ahead, then follow the
embankment to the right and, towards its end, bear left
to walk in the woods above some ruined buildings. Climb
ahead up through the remainder of the wood with the
buildings to your right. Cross the stile in the fence ahead,
cross the narrow field directly ahead to go down to cross
a footbridge and then climb some stone steps and a stile.
(300 metres)

ⓘ The embankment was of a reservoir that served the
buildings, the remains of an old cotton mill, with
waterpower. The mill burned down the mid-nineteenth
century. Some cottage walls also remain.

ⓧ In the next field follow the left-hand fence, by a former
lane, and continue in the same direction along the farm
track to arrive, through a gate, into the yard of (Little)
Catshaw Farm (1763). On your way a carved waymark

stone (a ram's head) is passed. Through the yard follow
the farm road and, at the junction turn right, and follow
the road into the yard of Catshaw Hall Farm (1678).
(850 metres)

The hall was an ancient manorial residence and, like
Hawthornthwaite, was listed in 1324 as a vaccary
(cattle farm) (see page 111). The building has charm
and vernacular interest and still contains some ancient
woodwork including a black oak staircase thought to be as
old as the house.

The gate facing you at the end of the yard leads you
into a field that you descend straight down by the left
hand hedgerow to a gated depression above some trees.
Go left through the gate, down an old track that heads
towards the river. Short of the river go left over a stile
in the fence, cross the footbridge over Hall Gill and then
follow the path along and right to go down to cross the
substantial Long Bridge over the River Wyre. (600 metres)

Whilst by the Wyre look for the white bib of the dipper or
watch it perched, bobbing on a river side boulder. Wagtails
or the flashing blue iridescence of the kingfisher may be
seen.

Over the footbridge cross the narrow field ahead, climb
the facing stile, go up the steps through the wood, and
then climb the stile at the top. Go ahead to cross the
track and follow, near the right-hand fence, to climb
steeply up the field. Pass through the right-hand of
two adjacent gates just to the left of a stile in the top
right-hand corner of the field and then follow along
the left-hand fence to a stile at the rear of Lentworth
House Farm. Continue directly ahead, and after passing
through the next two gates, emerge on the track by the

Abbeystead Reservoir

farmhouse. (500 metres) In the farmyard and alongside
the path can be found some interesting artistic features.

Opposite the end of the house cross the stile on
your right, (with an attractive rural-tool featured gate
adjacent to it) and follow the left-hand wall, noting the
weather vane with the way-mark stone (a duck) below it.
After the wall bends away left continue directly ahead,
heading for the distant grey barns, until the field dips
down via a carved stone (a bird), to where you cross
two consecutive stiles and a footbridge. Climb the field
to enter Wyresdale Churchyard by a gate and way-mark
stone (a bird of prey). (550 metres)

ⓘ Christ Church is the Shepherd's Church. It sits high above the Wyre with its gargoyle waterspouts leaning out from the squat tower of local stone. The church site dates back to at least the fourteenth century. The church was rebuilt in 1733, but when the estate passed to the Sefton family, it was extended. The pulpit dates from 1684. The church is usually locked but the vicarage lies adjacent (Tel 01524 792327). Inside the church porch you can see wooden bars with iron hooks used by the shepherds to hang their crooks and lanterns. The windows date from the turn of the century and represent biblical pastoral scenes but set in the local landscape. All feature sheep. On display is a 'Geneva' bible printed in 1599 being so named after the place where the bible was translated into English during times of persecution under Mary Tudor in this country. It is called the 'breeches bible' due to the modesty of the translators, as we read in Genesis 3 verse 7, that Adam and Eve made themselves breeches. Just above the church and vicarage is the Sunday School housed above the public stable. The original 1733 vicarage lies further to the north.

🚶 **Return to the gate by which you entered the churchyard and go half-left down the field again aiming for the grey roofed farm buildings to reach, in the bottom far corner of the field, a stile which you cross and then a footbridge. Climb up from the stream and go left by the old hedge line, again aiming for the grey barns, to a stile by a gate. Go over the stile and aim half-right to reach a stile in the right-hand edge of space between the buildings. Cross the concrete road beyond and go through the gate in the wall diagonally opposite. Cross this last field to a gate and stile in the far right-hand corner and then descend right along the road to Abbeystead and your start point. (750 metres)**

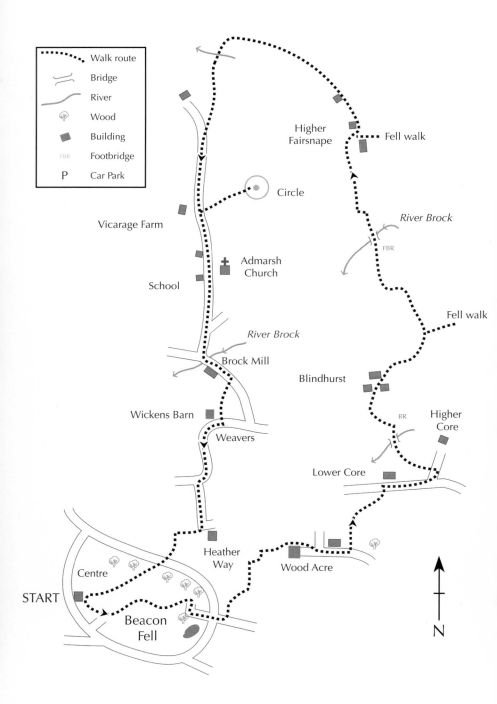

Walk route
Bridge
River
Wood
Building
FBR Footbridge
P Car Park

Higher
Fairsnape

Fell walk

Circle

River Brock

FBR

Vicarage Farm

Admarsh
Church

School

Fell walk

River Brock

Brock Mill

Blindhurst

Wickens Barn

Weavers

BR

Higher
Core

Lower Core

Heather
Way

Wood Acre

Centre

START

Beacon
Fell

N

WALK 17

Exploring Bleasdale from Beacon Fell

Exploring Bleasdale – from Beacon Fell

LENGTH:	13 km (8 miles)
START:	Visitor Centre on Beacon Fell (GR 565427)
BUS:	The nearest stop is Whitechapel on the 20 Garstang to Longridge and Goosnargh Thursday only service
PARKING:	In the vicinity of the Beacon Fell Country Park Visitor centre
MAP:	O.S. Explorer OL41 – Forest of Bowland & Ribblesdale

ℹ Whilst this walk starts and finishes near its highest point it affords excellent views of the Bowland fells, Pendle Hill, the Darwin Moors and Winter Hill. On a clear day the views of the Lakeland Hills and the Isle of Man can be superb. The walk around Bleasdale provides good views of this upland parish and an opportunity to visit the site of the Bleasdale Circle (see Walk 12 for details). A possible fellwalking extension is suggested for those suitably equipped. A walk we have used at all seasons of the year but perhaps Spring being the favourite time.

⊛ Take the slanting, cobbled path up from the visitor centre car park and, at its highest point, turn left to walk the surfaced path to the summit of the fell. The summit 'trig point' contains a viewpoint indicator. Turn right at the summit, go down through a small gate and follow the surfaced path down to eventually pass through another gate and emerge in the Quarry car park on the eastern side of the fell. Follow down the car park access road until you meet the road that circles the fell. (1.3 km)

Go left on the road and immediately turn right down Rigg Lane by the short left hand wall for 20 metres and

Beacon Fell

Gatekeeper

Brimstone

then climb the stile where the wall joins a fence. Go half-right down the field, aiming just right of Parlick Pike, to meet a gap between two fence corners in the bottom right-hand field corner. Ignore the stile to the right and go through the gap and continue down a sunken track beyond. This is often very wet and is followed near the left-hand fence over a footbridge and stile and then a redundant stile to the bottom left-hand corner of the field. There is a stile and gate on your left, which you do not cross, but just after the track has bent gently to the right go left over a further stile by a gate and walk down the next field by the left-hand boundary towards a further stile by a gate – but do not cross them. (1.1 km)

Instead turn right and follow the fence formerly facing you, and now on your left, pass over the stile by the gate seen ahead as you continue to the rear of the houses at Wood Acre. Just behind the houses cross the stile on your left and turn right along the fence to pass the end of the buildings and then climb the stile by the gate on your right. Go left down the access track to meet the road. Go right at this junction to Watery Gate Farm on your left. (500 metres)

Continue just past Watery Gate and go through the gate on your left just prior to the start of the narrow roadside wood. Go forward along the wood edge and then bear to the left to follow the left-hand fence along the field. Cross the stile in the fence facing you near the far left-hand field corner and then go half-right in the next field to reach the road by a gate opposite the barn of Lower Core Farm. The barn comes into view when crossing the field. Turn right and go up the road until you reach the gated access track to Lower Core Farm on your left. (1.2 km)

Go up the access track but leave it over the stile just beyond the first gate on your left. Follow near the right-hand wall and pass through the gateway in the

fenced section of field boundary near the right-hand
field corner. Cross the next field aiming for the nearby
Blindhurst Farm and, in a depression at the far side of
the field, cross the footbridge. Turn right in the next field
and follow near to the right-hand boundary until you see
a stile in a short section of stone wall. Cross the stile
and the subsequent footbridge and then cross the field
upwards to the access track and follow it up to the yard
of Blindhurst Farm. (950 metres)

ⓘ Blindhust farm has a 1731 datestone and its architectural
style, with cross windows and three-lighted mullion and
transomed windows, reflects the age of its construction.
There is another farmhouse to the left – it is said that two
brothers fought over the same land and when one brother
built a house, the other responded likewise.

Ⓚ Go to the right of the whitewashed farmhouse and
follow the track through two gates to emerge into a
small field. Turn immediately right and go up the field
to pass through a further gate. Go up near the right-
hand wall in the next field but then branch left along the
'concessionary' footpath that climbs a grassy track steeply
up to cross the stile by a gate. *For those with more
energy this concessionary path can be continued upwards
to the col to the north of Parlick. The ridge leads north
to the Paddy's Pole top of Fairsnape Fell from where a
further path leads down to Higher Fairsnape Farm and re-
connects with our route.* Our way goes to the left where
the descending track leads down to a fence alongside a
more conspicuous farm track. Cross the stile in the fence
facing you and then go down to a lower track that leads
right through a small stream. (500 metres)
    Just over the stream leave this track and go along the
left-hand fence, pass a gate, and climb the first stile. In
the next field descend right towards a small clump of

alder trees. Amidst this clump a footbridge takes you over the infant River Brock and then the path continues to cross a stile. In the next field follow the left-hand fence along to shortly reach a stile and a gate. Cross the stile, turn right and follow the track by the right-hand fence. This leads you through two gates with stiles and a third gate immediately below Higher Fairsnape Farm. Turn right up the access road to enter the farmyard through the gate, and continue left to pass the stone barn on your left and the two seventeenth century houses to your right. (1.2 km)

Higher Fairsnape is the possible site of vaccary (a medieval cattle farm). The date stone above the main house is very elaborate and is dated 1637 with the initials of the Parkinson family, the owners at that time.

Pass the left-hand barn and continue along the track, go through the gate facing you to a cobbled yard and then go to pass through the gate to the immediate right of the barn and re-enter fields. Continue along the distinct track by the left-hand fence through two fields. A gate, directly ahead, leads you into a third field but the track is less firm and you follow it down close to the left-hand wall. Leave this field by the gate facing you in the bottom left-hand field corner and then go down by the right-hand boundary to meet a track. (850 metres)

Turn left down the track, a 'concessionary' path, over the stream and then follow the left-hand fence to a gate and stile near Admarsh Barn Farm. Go over the stile and then left on the farm access road to pass the cattle-grid at Vicarage Farm (with access to Bleasdale Circle – see Walk 12) and then along and down past the church, school and village hall and continue over the next cattle grid and down to meet Bleasdale Lane. (2.5 km)

Go left to pass 'The Smithy' and climb up the road

until a flight of steps on your right leads you up to a stile and then into a field. Follow the left-hand boundary but, in the top left-hand field corner use the stile by the gate on your left to enter the field previously to your left. Turn right and follow the right-hand fence to a stile and a short enclosed path around the garden of Wickens Barn house to meet the road. Turn right on the road and, just after a sharp right-hand bend, go left down a long access track. When the track forks go directly ahead through the gate of Heatherway until you are opposite the house with its ugly large windows. (1.5 km)

Cross the stile by the gate on your left, follow the left-hand fence but after 100 metres go left, at a path junction by an over-head wire pole, and strike directly up the field to a stile below the trees of Beacon Fell. Cross the stile, go ahead to the road that circles the fell and cross it diagonally right to a forest track and barrier. Go up this track, pass to the immediate right of the lizard sculpture, and then through the small gate directly ahead to leave the forest. Go directly ahead on a path over the open fell to a small gate and short board-walk that lead into the next section of forest. Go straight ahead and follow the ruined left-hand wall down to the start at the information centre. (1.4 km)

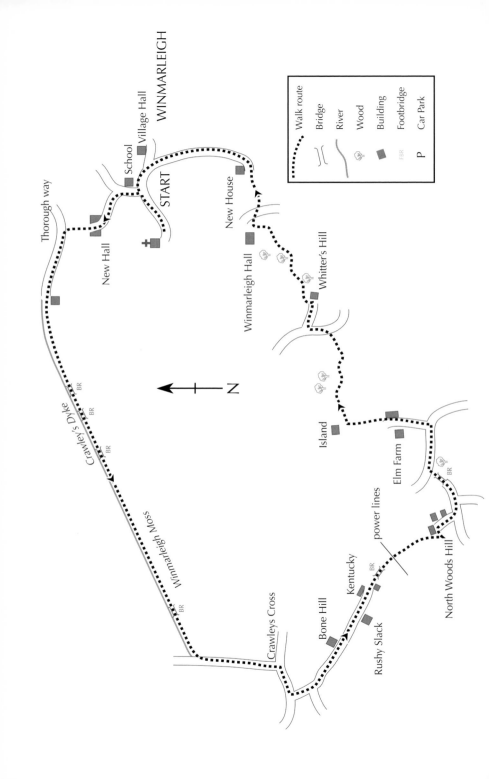

WALK 18

The Last of the Fylde Mosses

Winmarleigh – Bone Hill – Winmarleigh

LENGTH:	11.2 km (7 miles)
START:	Winmarleigh School (GR SD 472481)
BUS:	No suitable service
PARKING:	Not too easy, please park politely near Church, Village Hall or New House Lane
MAP:	O.S. Explorer 296 – Lancaster, Morecambe & Fleetwood

ⓘ This walk is virtually flat with the exception of the sporadic farmsteads being sited atop what once were minor islands in this former mossland landscape. The walk crosses the remnant of Winmarleigh Moss, a Site of Special Scientific Interest which reflects what much of the land between the current A6 and the coast must have looked like a few thousand years ago. The farm of Bone Hill, passed on the walk, has a dark history. Despite the low-lying position of the land it can provide a dry walk and, in season, there are some notable displays of snowdrops. In summer the vegetation can be rank in places, particularly where farmers have set aside land from production. At such times some paths can be hard to walk but the rewards of seeing butterflies and dragonflies can be very rewarding.

(🚶) From Winmarleigh School turn down School Lane and take the first left access road to reach New Hall Farm. Go through the cobbled farmyard with the farmhouse on your left and then go into a field by using the two gates facing you. Follow the field down to pass through the obvious gate in the boundary across your way. (1.0 km)

Go left on the track, called Thorough Way, and follow it all the way to the gas pipeline installation. The name of the track hints at an ancient route but its possible origins lie in the removal of peat from the mosses for use as litter for poultry houses in the late nineteenth century when two extraction companies were active. Cross the stile to the immediate right of the gate and follow between the right-hand dyke and the fenced site to enter the fields by a further stile by a gate. In the first field follow along beside the right-hand dyke to cross the stile by the gate in the far right-hand field corner. Continue in the same direction along the dyke in the next two fields, also by way of a stile and gate, and this leads to a footbridge in the far right-hand field corner. Use this to cross the main dyke coming from the left and then continue along the line of the right-hand dyke, as it becomes narrower, to cross a further footbridge in the far right-hand corner of the field. (2.0 km)

(ℹ️) The dyke we have been following is named Crawley's Dyke and later we come to Crawley's Cross Farm where lies Crawley's Cross, a boundary marker. The path continues, in the same direction, as close to the right-hand dyke across Winmarleigh Moss as the ground conditions allow. The path slightly wanders between tufty grasses and birch trees that are colonising the drying mossland. The peat soils are very evident. Heather and bog myrtle can be seen along with various birds. In summer watch out for butterflies, one day we saw twelve types on this walk, and dragonflies

Winmarleigh Moss

(🚶) Eventually the moss, across the dyke gives way to fields, and shortly you will reach a footbridge that enables you to leave the mossland. In the field continue to follow the right-hand boundary to a stile and gate in the far right-hand field corner and access to a track. (1.4 km of tough walking)

(🚶) Turn left on the track and then join the road by Crawley's Cross Farm. Turn right along the busy road but take the first left-hand turn into Bone Hill Lane. The Cross can be glimpsed in the ground of Crawley's Cross Cottage situated on the corner where you turn left. Go along this cul de sac, over the bridge, turn left at the junction and continue by way of Bone Hill until the track bends sharply right to Rushy Slack Farm. Leave the metalled lane here as our way continues straight ahead down the access track that leads to Kentucky Farm. Go straight ahead, with the houses to your left, and enter a field by the gate at the far end. (1.9 km)

(ℹ) Bone Hill Farm, the current house with a 1766 datestone, has a dark history for during the eighteenth and nineteenth century there lived a family whose notoriety, claims one historian, 'rivalled the Doones of Exmoor'. Amongst several infamous pursuits, it is claimed, the family ran a 'baby farm'. It was here that the embarrassment of the rich and noble families – the unwanted offspring of daughters and mistresses – were disposed of, or if the right fee was paid, reared to maturity. The head of the Bone Hill family, recognised by a white feather in his hat, would meet his clients in Garstang. Perhaps the path we now use was the way the mothers walked across the mosses to Bone Hill. The farm was also the site of a cock fighting main. A prehistoric bog burial was found in the vicinity of Bone Hill.

ⓧ Bear right in the field to find a footbridge across the
dyke behind the water-pumping site. In the next field (a
large arable field often planted with crops) aim towards
the left-hand corner of North Wood's Hill Farm. On the
way you pass under the overhead power cables almost
midway between two pylons. The old hedge line below
the farm is reached at a gateway beyond which the right-
of-way heads across towards the right-hand side of the
farm, enters the farmyard by a gate and goes left past the
front of the house. However, this may not be clear but
the track from the gateway follows the left-hand hedge
line and can be followed through the gated farmyard to
re-emerge by the farmhouse. From here go down the
short farm access road to the road, New Lane. (1.0 km)

Go left down the road and soon, where it bends right
to become Wood Lane, leave the road by going directly
ahead by the short farm track to cross a footbridge
adjacent to a farm-bridge and gate. Cross the next field
diagonally left by aiming for the white-gabled house and
go to pass through a gate with a prominent road sign
behind it. Turn right along the busy road, Black Lane,
but when it bends sharp right, go left down Station
Lane. This is named after the former Nateby Station and
the remains of the station platform can just be seen
in the garden of a bungalow on your right. Follow the
road along to Elm Farm and continue directly ahead,
sometimes with a barrier across the road. This is tractor
centre. Continue to pass the last building on your right
and, as the site road bends right go straight ahead, with a
hedge (whose abrupt end faces you) on your left, to enter
the fields by two consecutive gates. (1.0 km)

Go up the field by the left-hand hedge, go through the
gate facing you and continue by the left-hand hedge and
when this bends away to your left continue by aiming
directly for the gate below the houses at Island Farm. Go
through this gate turn right on the track with a left-hand

Towards the Bowland fells from near Winmarleigh

hedge and a right-hand fence. At the immediate end
of the fence go over the adjacent stile and continue by
the left-hand boundary and up by the left-hand wood.
Go down to the far left-hand field corner, turn to your
right in the same field and follow this boundary to pass
through the second of two gates on your left some
50 metres from the field corner. (700 metres)

Through this gate follow along the left-hand dyke side
all the way until you can leave the field by the facing
gate and stile. Go left along the road but soon turn right,
over a brick lined arched bridge, and follow the gated
access track that leads up to Whitters Hill, a private
house. On entering the gardens of the house turn left

and go between the boundary and the house to reach a high stile over a gate facing you. In the field go right and follow the right-hand boundary to pass a wood, a field boundary with a stile and then to reach the corner of the next wood. Go right through the metal swing gate and follow the path, enclosed between wire fences, round the edge of the wood, across fields and through another wood to eventually reach a metalled track. This path gives you a glimpse of the front of Winmarleigh Hall. (1.1 km)

ⓘ Paley designed Winmarleigh Hall in 1871 for the Patten Family from Warrington. The owner became the first, and the last, Lord Winmarleigh for ill luck dogged the family. The house was four-storeys, of red brick with a cloister like loggia. Partial rebuilding occurred after a fire in 1927.

Cross the track and go through a small gate. Bear slightly right amongst the planted trees and walk ahead in the field, with Nicky Nook in the distance and the farm roofs ahead, to cross a stile. Follow the right-hand fence down to cross a stile and through a gate to enter the yard of New House Farm. Go down through the yard to reach the road by way of the front of the farmhouse. Turn left along the road and keep left at the junction to return to your start. (1.1 km)

PUBLIC TRANSPORT

It is possible to undertake most, if not all, these walks with the use of public transport to the starting and finishing point. However, infrequent services calls for the necessity of careful planning if the services are to be used.

Prior to use of the services it is best to call the public transport information service, Traveline, on 0871 200 22 33. If you are calling from outside Lancashire ask for this county's service.

See also www.transportforlancashire.com

Bus Routes:

a) Services 40, 41, 42 operate between Lancaster, Garstang and Preston on a regular basis and serve walks 4, 5, 10, 11, 13, 15.

b) Service MO2 operates between Garstang, Myerscough College and Preston for walk 13.

c) Service 8C operates from Garstang to Calder Vale via Barnacre for walks 11 and 12.

d) Service 8K operates between Garstang and Knott End for walks 5, 7 and 8.

e) Service 8S operates between Garstang and Scorton for walk 3.

f) Service 86 operates between Knott End and Fleetwood for walks 7, 8 and 9.

g) Service 89 operates between Knott End and Lancaster for walks 8, 9,14 and 15.

h) Services 146 and 147 operate between Lancaster and Abbeystead serving walks 1, 2, 3, and 16.

i) Service 42 operates between Garstang and Blackpool for walks 4, 5, and 6.

j) The Knott End to Fleetwood Ferry, or a replacement bus service, serves walks 8 and 9.